Simple and Efficient Programming with C#

Skills to Build Applications with Visual Studio and .NET

Second Edition

Vaskaran Sarcar

Apress®

Simple and Efficient Programming with C#: Skills to Build Applications with Visual Studio and .NET

Vaskaran Sarcar
Kolkata, West Bengal, India

ISBN-13 (pbk): 978-1-4842-8736-1   ISBN-13 (electronic): 978-1-4842-8737-8
https://doi.org/10.1007/978-1-4842-8737-8

Managing Director, Apress Media LLC: Welmoed Spahr
Acquisitions Editor: Smriti Srivastava
Development Editor: Laura Berendson
Coordinating Editor: Mark Powers
Copy Editor: Kim Wimpsett

Cover designed by eStudioCalamar

Cover image designed by Vimal S on Unsplash (www.unsplash.com)

Distributed to the book trade worldwide by Apress Media, LLC, 1 New York Plaza, New York, NY 10004, U.S.A. Phone 1-800-SPRINGER, fax (201) 348-4505, e-mail orders-ny@springer-sbm.com, or visit www.springeronline.com. Apress Media, LLC is a California LLC and the sole member (owner) is Springer Science + Business Media Finance Inc (SSBM Finance Inc). SSBM Finance Inc is a **Delaware** corporation.

For information on translations, please e-mail booktranslations@springernature.com; for reprint, paperback, or audio rights, please e-mail bookpermissions@springernature.com.

Apress titles may be purchased in bulk for academic, corporate, or promotional use. eBook versions and licenses are also available for most titles. For more information, reference our Print and eBook Bulk Sales web page at www.apress.com/bulk-sales.

Any source code or other supplementary material referenced by the author in this book is available to readers on GitHub (https://github.com/Apress). For more detailed information, please visit www.apress.com/source-code.

Printed on acid-free paper

I dedicate this book to the programming lovers of C#.

Table of Contents

About the Author

 **Vaskaran Sarcar** obtained his master's degree in software engineering from Jadavpur University, Kolkata (India), and his MCA from Vidyasagar University, Midnapore (India). He was a National Gate Scholar (2007–2009) and has more than 12 years of experience in education and the IT industry. Vaskaran devoted his early career (2005–2007) to the teaching profession at various engineering colleges, and later he joined HP India PPS R&D Hub Bangalore. He worked there until August 2019. At the time of his retirement from HP, he was a senior software engineer and team lead. To follow his dream and passion, Vaskaran is now an independent full-time author. Other Apress books by Vaskaran include:

- *Test your Skills in C# Programming* (Apress, 2022)
- *Java Design Patterns, Third Edition* (Apress, 2022)
- *Simple and Efficient Programming in C#* (Apress, 2021)
- *Design Patterns in C#, Second Edition* (Apress, 2020)
- *Getting Started with Advanced C#* (Apress, 2020)
- *Interactive Object-Oriented Programming in Java, Second Edition* (Apress, 2019)
- *Java Design Patterns, Second Edition* (Apress, 2019)
- *Design Patterns in C#* (Apress, 2018)
- *Interactive C#* (Apress, 2017)
- *Interactive Object-Oriented Programming in Java* (Apress, 2016)
- *Java Design Patterns* (Apress, 2016)

The following are other books he's written:

- *Python Bookcamp* (Amazon, 2021)
- *Operating System: Computer Science Interview Series* (Createspace, 2014)

About the Technical Reviewers

Shekhar Kumar Maravi is a lead engineer in design and development whose main interests are programming languages, algorithms, and data structures. He obtained his master's degree in computer science and engineering from the Indian Institute of Technology – Bombay. After graduation, he joined Hewlett-Packard's R&D Hub in India to work on printer firmware. Currently he is a technical lead engineer for automated pathology lab diagnostic devices at Siemens Healthcare R&D division. He can be reached by email at shekhar.maravi@gmail.com or via LinkedIn at www.linkedin.com/in/shekharmaravi.

Carsten Thomsen is a back-end developer primarily but works with smaller front-end bits as well. He has authored and reviewed a number of books and created numerous Microsoft Learning courses, all to do with software development. He works as a freelancer/contractor in various countries in Europe, using Azure, Visual Studio, Azure DevOps, and GitHub. He also enjoys working with architecture, research, analysis, development, testing, and bug fixing.

Introduction

It is my absolute pleasure to write the second edition of *Simple and Efficient Programming with C#: Skills to Build Applications with Visual Studio and .NET*. You can surely guess that I got this opportunity because you liked the previous edition of the book and shared your feedback with us. So, once again I'm excited to join you and help you to learn more. This time I present a further simplified, better organized, and more content-rich edition to you.

Let me remind you of the key goals of this book. I wrote about them in the first edition as well. C# is an object-oriented programming (OOP) language. You may already know C# keywords or even some interesting features. You may also know how to write simple programs in C#. You can learn these things from an introductory book or an online tutorial. These are useful things to know, but they are not sufficient to understand an enterprise codebase. This is why a novice programmer often finds it difficult to understand an expert's code. They may wonder why an experienced programmer wrote the program in a particular way. It may appear to the novice that the expert could have used an easier approach to solve the problem. But there are reasons why an experienced programmer might follow a different approach. The word *experienced* indicates that these programmers have more experience in programming and know the pros and cons of different approaches. They know how the C# features can be used in the best possible way to develop an application. So, the applications they make are usually powerful. What do I mean by a powerful application? For me, a powerful application is robust, extensible, and easily maintainable, but simple to use. This book is an introductory guide for developing such applications. This was the core aim of this book.

To write better-quality programs, senior programmers follow experts' footprints. They learn from the collective wisdom and recorded experience of the past. So, instead of attempting an entirely new solution, you should first consider this knowledge base, which will help you produce better-quality code. It is always better if you know about why you should or shouldn't follow any specific guideline.

Malcolm Gladwell, in his book *Outliers* (Little, Brown and Company), discussed the 10,000-hour rule. This rule says that the key to achieving world-class expertise in any skill is, to a large extent, a matter of practicing the correct way, for a total of around

10,000 hours. I acknowledge that it is impossible to consider all experiences before you write a program. Also, sometimes it is OK to bend the rules if the return on investment (ROI) is nice. So, keep in mind the Pareto principle, or the 80-20 rule. This rule simply states that 80 percent of outcomes come from 20 percent of all causes. This is useful in programming too. When you identify the most essential characteristics of top-quality programs and use them in your applications, you also qualify yourself as an experienced programmer, and your application will be robust, flexible, and maintainable. In this book, I share with you these important principles using some case studies, which will help you write better programs. Some of these principles you may know already, but when you see them in action and compare these case studies, you'll understand their importance.

So, what is new in this second edition? Well, the first thing I want to tell you is that this edition maintains the same goals that were mentioned in the first edition. Second, you can easily guess that it is a further simplified, enlarged, and polished version. This time you see the use of top-level statements throughout the book. You may know that top-level statements have been supported since C# 9.0. In addition, the .NET 6+ project template for C# console apps uses top-level statements. At the time of this writing, C# 11 is not released, but you can test the preview features. I have taken this opportunity to use some of them, particularly **raw-string literals**. I talk about static abstract interface members too. I used many preview features in my other book, *Test Your Skills in C# Programming*. But for this book, not all of them are required.

Additionally, this is an expanded edition. Two new chapters in Part IV, Chapter 10 and Chapter 11, talk about handling errors in a better way. Particularly, you'll see a discussion of organizing exceptions and handling null values with different case studies.

How Is the Book Organized?

The book has five major parts, which are as follows:

- The first three chapters form **Part I**, in which there is a detailed discussion of polymorphism and the use of abstract classes and interfaces. Here, code comments will be examined, and you will learn when to use them effectively. These are the fundamental building blocks for the rest of the book.

- In the world of programming, there is no shortage of programming principles and design guidelines. Each of these suggestions has its own benefits. To become a professional programmer, you do not need to learn everything at the same time. In **Part II**, I discuss six design principles, which include the SOLID principles and the DRY principle. These are the foundation of well-known design patterns.

- The best way to learn is by doing and analyzing case studies. So, in **Part III** of the book, you will see interesting applications that use some well-known patterns. This part gives you hints about how a professional coder develops an enterprise application.

- Handling errors is an unavoidable part of programming. Particularly, runtime exceptions are dangerous, and often they appear in the form of NullReferenceException in C#. **Part IV** focuses on them, discusses different case studies with easy-to-understand examples, and provides useful suggestions about possible improvements.

- There is no end to learning. So, **Part V** includes some interesting topics such as how to prevent memory leaks, how to choose between a static method and an instance method, and some common terms from software development that are not discussed in detail in this book. A quick overview of these topics will help your future learnings and experiments.

- You can download all the source codes for the book from the publisher's website. I have a plan to maintain the "errata," and, if required, I can also make some updates/announcements there. So, I suggest you visit those pages to receive any important corrections or updates.

Prerequisite Knowledge

This book is intended for those who are familiar with the common language constructs of C# and have a basic understanding of pure object-oriented concepts such as polymorphism, inheritance, abstraction, encapsulation, and, most importantly, how to compile or run a C# application in Visual Studio. This book does not invest time in easily available topics, such as how to install Visual Studio on your system, how to write a "Hello World" program in C#, how you can use an `if-else` statement or a `while` loop, etc. This book is written using the most basic features of C# so that for most of the programs herein you do not need to be familiar with advanced topics in C#. The examples are simple, and I believe that they are written in such a way that even if you are familiar with another popular language such as Java, C++, and so on, you can still easily grasp the concepts in this book.

Who Is This Book For?

In short, you can pick up this book if the answer is "yes" to the following questions:

- Are you familiar with basic constructs in C# and object-oriented concepts such as polymorphism, inheritance, abstraction, and encapsulation?

- Do you know how to set up your coding environment?

- Have you completed at least one introductory course on C# and now are interested in writing better programs?

- Are you also interested to know how a professional programmer designs their applications?

You probably shouldn't pick this book if the answer is yes to any of the following questions:

- Are you absolutely new to C#?

- Are you looking for advanced concepts in C#, excluding the topics mentioned previously?

- Are you interested in exploring a book where the focus is not on standard design principles?

- Do you not like Windows, Visual Studio, and/or .NET and want to learn and use C# without them?

Guidelines for Using This Book

To use this book more effectively, consider the following:

- This book works best if you've gone through an introductory course on C# and are familiar with the common terms, such as polymorphism, and have heard about abstract classes and interfaces. If this is not the case, please read about these topics before you start reading this book.

- I suggest you go through the chapters sequentially. This is because some fundamental design techniques may have been discussed in a previous chapter, and I have not repeated those techniques in later chapters.

- I started this book using **Microsoft Visual Studio Community 2022 in a Windows 10 environment**. This community edition is free of charge. When I started the book, I started with the latest versions of C# that were available at that time. You can easily guess that version updates kept coming, so I kept updating my code repository. When I finished my first draft, I had the most recent version of Visual Studio Community 2022 (version **17.3.3**). Almost in every case, my target framework was **.NET 7.0**, which supports **C# 11**.

- In this context, it is useful to know that nowadays the C# language version is automatically selected based on your project's target framework(s), so you can always get the highest compatible version by default.

- For example, C# 11 is for .NET 7 and later versions. Similarly, C# 10 is supported only on .NET 6 and newer versions. C# 9 is supported only on .NET 5 and newer versions. C# 8.0 is supported only on .NET Core 3.x and newer versions. If you are interested in the C# language versioning, you can go to this link: `https://docs.microsoft.com/en-us/dotnet/csharp/language-reference/configure-language-version`.

- The fact is that these version updates will come continuously, but I strongly believe that these version details should not matter much to you because I have used the fundamental constructs of C#. So, the code in this book should execute smoothly in the upcoming versions of C#/Visual Studio as well. Though I also believe that the results should not vary in other environments, you know the nature of software—it is naughty. So, I recommend that if you want to see the exact same output, you mimic the same environment.

- If you do not use the Windows operating system, you can use Visual Studio Code, which is also a source-code editor developed by Microsoft to support Windows, Linux, or Mac operating systems. This multiplatform IDE is also free.

- You can download and install the Visual Studio IDE from `https://visualstudio.microsoft.com/downloads/`. You will the screen shown in Figure I-1.

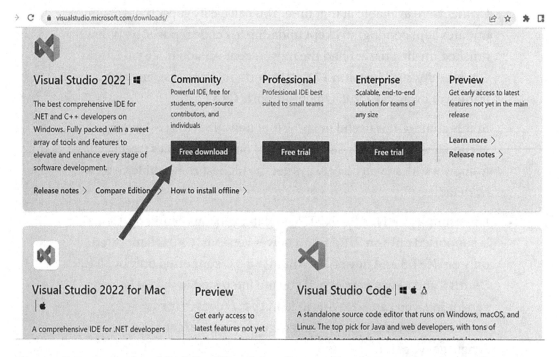

Figure I-1. *Download link for Visual Studio 2022 and Visual Studio Code*

Note At the time of writing, this information is correct. But the link and policies may change in the future.

- I have also installed the class designer component in Visual Studio 2022 to draw class diagrams for my programs. They'll help you understand the code better.

Conventions Used in This Book

All the output and code of the book follow the same font and structure. To draw your attention to some places, I have made them bold. For example, consider the following code fragment and the lines in bold (taken from Chapter 4 when I discuss the LSP):

```
// The previous codes are skipped

// Instantiating two registered users
RegisteredUser robin = new("Robin");
RegisteredUser jack = new("Jack");
helper.AddUser(robin);
helper.AddUser(jack);

GuestUser guestUser1 = new();
helper.AddUser(guestUser1);

// Processing the payments using
// the helper class.
// You can see the problem now.
helper.ShowPreviousPayments();
helper.ProcessNewPayments();

// The remaining codes are skipped
```

Final Words

You are an intelligent person. You have chosen a subject that can assist you throughout your career. As you learn about these concepts, I suggest you write your own code; only then will you master this area. There is no shortcut to true learning. In a similar context, can you remember Euclid's (the ancient Greek mathematician who is often considered the father of geometry) reply to the ruler? If not, let me remind you of his reply: "There is no royal road to geometry." Similarly, in programming, there is no shortcut. So, study and code; understand a new concept and code again. Do not give up when you face challenges. They are the indicators that you are growing better.

I believe that this book is designed for you in such a way that upon its completion, you will develop an adequate knowledge of the topic, and, most importantly, you'll know how to go further. Lastly, I hope that this book can provide help to you and that you will value the effort.

PART I

Fundamentals

Part I consists of three chapters, in which we will discuss the following questions:

- How can we use the power of polymorphism, and why is it beneficial?

- How can we combine an abstract class and interfaces to make an efficient application?

- How can we use meaningful code comments and avoid unnecessary comments in a program?

Almost every C# application uses comments, the concept of polymorphism, and abstract classes and interfaces. When we implement these techniques in a better way, the program is better. I consider them the fundamental techniques for an efficient application.

CHAPTER 1

Flexible Code Using Polymorphism

Ask a developer the following question: "What are the fundamental characteristics of object-oriented programming (OOP)?" You will hear an immediate reply saying that classes (and objects), inheritance, abstraction, encapsulation, and polymorphism are the most important characteristics of OOP. In addition, when you analyze OOP-based enterprise code, you'll find different forms of polymorphism. But the truth is that a novice programmer rarely uses the power of polymorphism. Why? It is said that object-oriented programmers pass through three important stages. In the first stage, they become familiar with non-object-oriented constructs. In this stage, they use decision statements, looping constructs, etc. In the second stage, they start creating classes and objects and use the inheritance mechanism. Finally, in the third stage, they use polymorphism to achieve late binding and make their programs flexible. But writing the polymorphic is not always easy. Honestly, it is a little bit tough compared to the other features of OOP. Using some simple but powerful code examples, this chapter will make this concept easy for you to understand.

Recap of Polymorphism

Polymorphism simply means there is *one name with many forms.* In the real world, it is a common phenomenon. Consider the behavior of your pet dog: when it sees an unknown person, it starts barking. But when it sees you, it makes different noises and behaves differently. In both cases, this dog sees with its eyes, but based on the observation, the dog behaves differently.

© Vaskaran Sarcar 2023
V. Sarcar, *Simple and Efficient Programming with C#*, https://doi.org/10.1007/978-1-4842-8737-8_1

You can relate this concept to other areas as well. For example, consider the customer support departments in different organizations. They each provide support to the customers in their own way. Similarly, each of the search engine providers such as Google, Yahoo, or Microsoft Bing searches the Internet following its own algorithm.

OOP likes to mimic real-world scenarios, and conceptually, the polymorphic code works in the same way. In C#, a class can have methods (or properties). Optionally, you can provide implementations for them. C# also allows the derived classes to override those implementations as per their needs. As a result, these related types can have methods with the same name, but they can show different behaviors. This is the key concept to understand before you deal with the polymorphic code.

Initial Program

The importance of a feature is often realized in the absence of it. So, I start with a program that does not use the concept of polymorphism. This program compiles and runs successfully. Here you have three different types of animals—tigers, dogs, and monkeys. Each of them can produce a different sound. So, I made classes with their corresponding names, and in each class, you see a Sound() method. Check whether you can improve this program.

Demonstration 1

Here is the complete demonstration:

```
Console.WriteLine("***Sounds of the different animals.***");
Tiger tiger = new();
tiger.Sound();
Dog dog = new();
dog.Sound();
Monkey monkey = new();
monkey.Sound();
Console.ReadKey();
class Tiger
{
    public void Sound()
    {
```

```
        Console.WriteLine("Tigers roar.");
    }
}
class Dog
{
    public void Sound()
    {
        Console.WriteLine("Dogs bark.");
    }
}
class Monkey
{
    public void Sound()
    {
        Console.WriteLine("Monkeys whoop.");
    }
}
```

Output

Here is the output:

```
***Sounds of the different animals.***
Tigers roar.
Dogs bark.
Monkeys whoop.
```

Analysis

I have used the simplified new expressions here. For example, the line Tiger tiger = new(); is the simplified version of Tiger tiger = new Tiger(); Starting with C# 9.0, you can use this form. It says that during the constructor invocation if the target type of an expression is known, you can omit the type name.

When you use Tiger tiger = new Tiger();, the tiger is a reference to an object that is based on the Tiger class. This reference refers to the object, but it does not contain the object data itself. Even Tiger tiger; is a valid line of code that creates an object reference without creating the actual object.

Understand that when you use `Tiger tiger = new Tiger();`, we say that ***you are programming to an implementation***. Notice that in this case the reference and object both are of the same type. You can improve this program using the concept of polymorphism. In the upcoming implementation, I show you such an example. I use an interface in this example. Before I show you the example, let me remind you of a few important points:

- I could achieve the same effect using an abstract class. When you use an abstract class or an interface, the first thing that comes to mind is inheritance. How do you know whether you are correctly using inheritance? The simple answer is that you do an IS-A test. For example, a rectangle IS-A shape, but the reverse is not necessarily true. Take another example: a monkey IS-An animal, but not all animals are monkeys. Notice that the IS-A test is unidirectional.

- In programming, if you inherit class B from class A, you say that B is the subclass and A is the parent class or base class. **But most importantly, you can say B is a type of A**. So, if you derive a `Tiger` class or a `Dog` class from a base class called `Animal` (or an interface say `IAnimal`), you can say that `Dog` IS-An `Animal` (or `IAnimal`) or `Tiger` IS-An `Animal` (or `IAnimal`). Similarly, a rectangle IS-A special type of shape. A square IS-A special type of rectangle. So, a square IS-A shape too.

- If you have an inheritance tree, this IS-A test can be applied anywhere in the tree.

- Let us assume that I represent rectangles and shapes using the `Rectangle` and `Shape` classes, respectively. Now when I say `Rectangle` IS-A `Shape`, programmatically I tell that a `Rectangle` instance can invoke the methods that a `Shape` instance can invoke. But, if needed, a `Rectangle` class can include some specific methods that are absent in the `Shape` class. To invoke these specific methods, you need to use a `Rectangle` instance only; since the `Shape` class does not include those methods, the `Shape` instances cannot call them.

In C#, a parent (or base) class reference can refer to a subclass object. Since each `tiger`, `dog`, or `monkey` is an animal, you can introduce a parent type and inherit all these concrete classes from it. I told you that I am going to use a C# interface now. Following the C# naming convention, let's name the supertype as `IAnimal`.

Here is a code fragment that shows the IAnimal interface. It also gives you an idea of how to override its Sound() method in the Tiger class. The Monkey and Dog class can do the same thing.

```
interface IAnimal
{
    void Sound();
}
class Tiger : IAnimal
{
    public void Sound()
    {
        Console.WriteLine("Tigers roar.");
    }
}
```

Programming to a supertype gives you more flexibility. It allows you to use a reference variable polymorphically. The following code segment demonstrates such a usage:

```
IAnimal animal = new Tiger();
animal.Sound();
animal = new Dog();
animal.Sound();
// The remaining code skipped
```

Better Program

Now I rewrite this program which produces the same output. Let's take a look at the following demonstration.

Demonstration 2

Here is demonstration 2. It is a modified version of demonstration 1.

```
Console.WriteLine("***Sounds of the different animals.***");

IAnimal animal = new Tiger();
animal.Sound();
animal = new Dog();
animal.Sound();
animal = new Monkey();
animal.Sound();

interface IAnimal
{
    void Sound();
}
class Tiger : IAnimal
{
    public void Sound()
    {
        Console.WriteLine("Tigers roar.");
    }
}
class Dog : IAnimal
{
    public void Sound()
    {
        Console.WriteLine("Dogs bark.");
    }
}
class Monkey : IAnimal
{
    public void Sound()
    {
        Console.WriteLine("Monkeys whoop.");
    }
}
```

Analysis

Have you noticed the difference? This time I used the superclass reference `animal` to refer to different derived class objects.

Following this approach, not only do you type less, but you also use a program that is more flexible and easier to maintain. If needed, now you can iterate over a list too. For example, you can replace the following code segment inside `Main()`:

```
IAnimal animal = new Tiger();
animal.Sound();
animal = new Dog();
animal.Sound();
animal = new Monkey();
animal.Sound();
```

with the following code:

```
List<IAnimal> animals = new List<IAnimal>
{
    new Tiger(),
    new Dog(),
    new Monkey()
};

foreach (IAnimal animal in animals)
    animal.Sound();
```

If you run the program again with these changes, you see the same output.

Notice that in demonstration 1, when a client reads the line `dog.Sound()`, they can assume that the `Sound()` method from the `Dog` class will be invoked.

But in demonstration 2, when the client reads the line `animal.Sound()`, it is not obvious which subtype of `IAnimal` will invoke the `Sound()`. Why is this important? As a programmer, you do not provide every possible detail to your clients.

This discussion is not over yet. Here I have used one of the simplest forms of polymorphism. In this case, a question may come to mind: we know a supertype reference can refer to a subtype object in C#. So, when I use the following lines:

```
IAnimal animal = new Tiger();
animal.Sound();
```

9

you can surely predict that the Sound() method of Tiger class will be used. So, it appears that you know the output in advance and you doubt the concept of polymorphism. If this is the case, let us further dig into this.

Let us assume that you create a subtype based on some runtime random number generator (or user input). In this case, you cannot predict the output in advance. For example, see the following lines of code:

```
IAnimal animal = AnimalProducer.GetAnimal();
animal.Sound();
```

What is the difference? Anyone who sees this code segment can assume that GetAnimal() of the AnimalProducer class returns an animal that can make some sound. How can you achieve this? It is pretty simple: let me rewrite the program. Notice the changes in bold:

```
Console.WriteLine("***Sounds of the different animals.***");
IAnimal animal = AnimalProducer.GetAnimal();
animal.Sound();
animal = AnimalProducer.GetAnimal();
animal.Sound();
animal = AnimalProducer.GetAnimal();
animal.Sound();

interface IAnimal
{
    void Sound();
}
class Tiger : IAnimal
{
    public void Sound()
    {
        Console.WriteLine("Tigers roar.");
    }
}
class Dog : IAnimal
{
```

```csharp
    public void Sound()
    {
        Console.WriteLine("Dogs bark.");
    }
}
class Monkey : IAnimal
{
    public void Sound()
    {
        Console.WriteLine("Monkeys whoop.");
    }
}

class AnimalProducer
{
    internal static IAnimal GetAnimal()
    {
        IAnimal animal;
        Random random = new Random();
        // Get a number between 0 and 3(exclusive)
        int temp = random.Next(0, 3);

        if (temp == 0)
        {
            animal = new Tiger();
        }
        else if (temp == 1)
        {
            animal = new Dog();
        }
        else
        {
            animal = new Monkey();
        }
        return animal;
    }
}
```

Run this application now and notice the output. Here is the sample output that I got on the various runs:

First Run:

```
***Sounds of the different animals.***
Monkeys whoop.
Dogs bark.
Monkeys whoop.
```

Second Run:

```
***Sounds of the different animals.***
Dogs bark.
Dogs bark.
Tigers roar.
```

Third Run:

```
***Sounds of the different animals.***
Tigers roar.
Monkeys whoop.
Dogs bark.
```

It is now clear that no one can predict the output of this program in advance. You can see the effective use of polymorphism in this example.

POINTS TO REMEMBER

If you like to shorten this code, instead of using the `if-else` chain, you can use the `switch` expression as follows:

```
animal =
temp switch
{
  0 => new Tiger(),
  1 => new Dog(),
  _ => new Monkey()
};
```

One more point: you can use a simplified new expression again. For example, the line Random random = new Random(); can be shortened if you use Random random = new();. When you download the source code from the Apress website, refer to the folder Demo3_ Polymorphism inside Chapter1 to see the complete program.

Now I'll show you some code that helps you understand and use polymorphic code in an alternative way. You can replace animal.Sound(); with the following code:

```
AnimalProducer.MakeSound(animal);
```

MakeSound() is defined inside the AnimalProducer class as follows:

```
internal static void MakeSound(IAnimal animal)
{
  animal.Sound();
}
```

Why am I showing this to you? Following this approach, you can pass a supertype reference to this method to invoke the appropriate subtype method. This also gives you flexibility and helps you write better, more readable code. Here is an alternative version of the program that we have just discussed:

```
Console.WriteLine("***Sounds of the different animals.***");
IAnimal animal = AnimalProducer.GetAnimal();
AnimalProducer.MakeSound(animal);
animal = AnimalProducer.GetAnimal();
AnimalProducer.MakeSound(animal);
animal = AnimalProducer.GetAnimal();
AnimalProducer.MakeSound(animal);

interface IAnimal
{
    void Sound();
}
class Tiger : IAnimal
{
    public void Sound()
    {
```

```
            Console.WriteLine("Tigers roar.");
    }
}
class Dog : IAnimal
{
    public void Sound()
    {
        Console.WriteLine("Dogs bark.");
    }
}
class Monkey : IAnimal
{
    public void Sound()
    {
        Console.WriteLine("Monkeys whoop.");
    }
}

class AnimalProducer
{
    internal static IAnimal GetAnimal()
    {
        IAnimal animal;
        Random random = new Random();
        // Get a number between 0 and 3(exclusive)
        int temp = random.Next(0, 3);

        animal =
        temp switch
        {
            0 => new Tiger(),
            1 => new Dog(),
            _ => new Monkey()
        };

        return animal;
    }
```

```
internal static void MakeSound(IAnimal animal)
{
    animal.Sound();
}
}
```

Note   You should not assume that the GetAnimal() and MakeSound(...)
methods need to be static only. You can use them as instance methods too. When
you download the source code from the Apress website, refer to the folder Demo4_
Polymorphism inside Chapter1 to see this modified program.

Useful Notes

Before I finish this chapter, let me point out some important information for your
immediate reference.

C# types including the user-defined types are polymorphic because they inherit
from Object.

To implement a polymorphic behavior, I started with an interface. I could achieve
the same result using an abstract class. In this case, you'd use the abstract and override
keywords in the respective code segments. Here is a sample:

```
abstract class Animal
{
    public abstract void Sound();
}
class Tiger : Animal
{
    public override void Sound()
    {
        Console.WriteLine("Tigers roar.");
    }
}
```

But when you use a concrete parent class and want its derived classes to redefine its method(s), you see the use of virtual keywords in the parent class. Here is a sample:

```
class Animal
{
    public virtual void Sound()
    {
        Console.WriteLine("I make sounds.");
    }
}
class Tiger : Animal
{
    public override void Sound()
    {
        Console.WriteLine("Tigers roar.");
    }
}
```

In short, a base class can define (or implement) virtual methods, and if needed, the derived classes override them as per their needs. As a result, at runtime, when client code calls the method, the common language runtime (CLR) can invoke the appropriate method based on the runtime type of the object. These are the key things to understand in the polymorphic code.

Note   C# primarily supports OOP. But being hybrid in nature, it can support functional programming (FP) too. FP prefers immutability and pure functions. A function is pure if it returns the same value for the same input. Otherwise, it is an impure function. So, from a FP developer's point of view, you may consider the dynamic behavior of a method as a problem instead of an advantage. But I remind you that our focus is on OOP in this book, but not on FP. So, you should not be confused.

In this chapter, I discussed the code examples using C# interfaces. So, I'd like to point out one important change that came in C# 11. Consider the following code:

```
Console.WriteLine("Testing a C#11 feature");
public interface ISample
{
    static abstract void ShowInterfaceName();
}
```

If you run this code in C# 10, you'll see the compile-time error. Here is a sample:

```
CS8703 The modifier 'abstract' is not valid for this item in C# 10.0.
Please use language version 'preview' or greater.
```

This message is self-explanatory. So, you need to understand that this feature was planned for C# 11. At the same time, you also need to remember that only interface members that aren't fields can be static abstract. So, if you write something like the following:

```
public interface ISample
{
    static abstract int SomeFlag; // ERROR CS0681
}
```

you'll see the following error: CS0681 The modifier 'abstract' is not valid on fields. Try using a property instead.

In short, you can refer to the following code segment and keep the supporting comments in mind when you use a C# interface in your program:

```
public interface ISample
{
    //static abstract int SomeFlag1; // ERROR CS0681
    static int SomeFlag2=1; // OK, but warning message
                        // (CA 2211)
    // Interfaces cannot contain instance fields
    int _someFlag3; // ERROR CS0525
    const int SomeFlag3 = 3; // OK
    static abstract void ShowInterfaceName1(); // OK in C#11
    void ShowInterfaceName2(); // OK
}
```

Summary

To implement polymorphic behavior, I started with an interface. I could achieve the same effect using an abstract class. There are situations when an interface is a better choice over an abstract class, and vice versa. You will see a discussion about this in Chapter 2.

When you code to a parent type (it can be an interface, an abstract class, or simply a parent class), the code can work with any new classes implementing the interface. This helps you to adjust to lots of new changes in the future, and you can adopt those requirements easily. This is the power of polymorphism. But if you use only concrete classes in your program, it is likely that you may need to change your existing code in the future such as when you add a new concrete class. This approach does not follow the Open/Closed principle, which says your code should be open for extension but closed for modification.

I have shown you the advantages of polymorphism. But it's not always easy to write polymorphic code, and you need to be careful when you use it. You'll get a better idea about this when I discuss SOLID principles in Chapter 4.

Everything in this chapter may not be new to you, but I believe that you have a better idea about polymorphism now. Before you move on to the next chapters, let me make sure that we agree on the following points.

When you write the following:

```
Tiger tiger = new Tiger();
tiger.Sound();
```

you are programming to concrete implementation.

When you write the following:

```
IAnimal animal = new Tiger();
animal.Sound();
```

you are programming to a supertype. It is often referred to as *programming to an interface*.

Note   When we say *programming to an interface*, it does not necessarily mean that you use a C# interface only. It can be an abstract class or a parent/base class too.

You can follow a better approach when you write something like this:

```
IAnimal animal = AnimalProducer.GetAnimal();
animal.Sound();
```

In this case, by merely reading the code, no one can predict the output in advance. In simple terms, this code segment implies that you announce to the outside world that you get an animal through the GetAnimal() method and this animal can make a sound.

In short, this chapter answered the following questions:

- How can you perform an IS-A test?

- How can you write a polymorphic code for your application, and why is it better?

- How can you iterate over a list when you write the polymorphic code?

- How can you write a better polymorphic code?

- How do experts differentiate between "programming to an implementation" and "programming to an interface"?

CHAPTER 2

Abstract Class or Interface?

There are many code segments in which you can use an abstract class instead of a C# interface and vice versa. If the code is small and is used to perform a simple task, you may not see the difference between these two techniques. On the contrary, when the code is big and extendable, the choice between them can play a vital role in performance and maintenance.

This chapter doesn't focus on the basic differences between an abstract class and an interface. Instead, I'll show some code segments where you can use either of them and the compiler does not raise any issues. Then we will analyze how to write an efficient program combining both these techniques in some specific scenarios.

Recap of Abstract Classes and Interfaces

Before I talk about the fundamental differences between an abstract class and an interface, let me remind you of some important points to avoid some common confusion in the future.

- Normally an abstract class suits best when you share a common behavior across subclasses but you guarantee that nobody can make an object from the class.

- The interfaces are best when you define some "roles" that other classes play and it does not matter whether these classes belong to the same inheritance tree or not. What does this mean? See the following discussion.

© Vaskaran Sarcar 2023
V. Sarcar, *Simple and Efficient Programming with C#*, https://doi.org/10.1007/978-1-4842-8737-8_2

In Figure 2-1, you can see that the `Tiger` and `Dog` classes inherit from the abstract class `Animal`. There is a `Sound()` method in these classes.

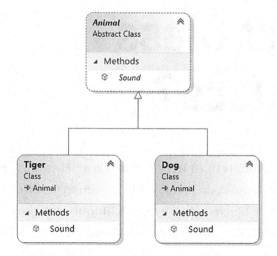

Figure 2-1. *Animal hierarchy*

In Figure 2-2, you can see that the `TigerToy` class and `JumpingDog` class inherit from the `SoftToys` class. Each class in this inheritance hierarchy contains a `Sound()` method too.

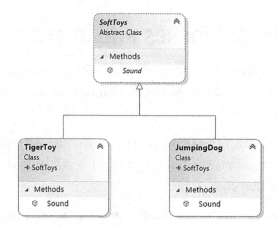

Figure 2-2. *SoftToys hierarchy*

Now tell me, though all of the `Tiger`, `Dog`, `TigerToy`, and `JumpingDog` instances can make sound, should you mix them? Or, can you say soft toys are animals or that animals are soft toys? No.

This is because the animal hierarchy and the soft toy hierarchy are different. You cannot treat a jumping dog (which is a soft toy) as a living animal only because it can make a sound.

But an interface can fit in this scenario. If you start with an interface, say, ISound, the Tiger class, Dog class, TigerToy class, and JumpingDog class can all implement the interface and override the Sound() method as per their need.

- An abstract class has its own power and uses. For example, it can contain fields and concrete methods that an interface cannot contain. From C# 8 on, you can include default methods in an interface. But normally an interface is like an abstract class that includes all the abstract methods.

- In short, when you need to simulate the behaviors from multiple classes, an interface is the right choice. This is because C# does not support the concept of multiple inheritances through classes.

DIAMOND PROBLEM

Suppose there is an inheritance hierarchy in which the Shape class is placed on top. This class has a method called AboutMe(). Two classes, Triangle and Rectangle, derive from Shape. Both derived classes have redefined the AboutMe() method (in programming terms, they have overridden the method as per their needs). The code may look like this:

```
class Shape
    {
        public virtual void AboutMe()
        {
            Console.WriteLine("It is an arbitrary Shape.");
        }
    }
    class Triangle : Shape
    {
```

```
        public override void AboutMe()
        {
            Console.WriteLine("It is a Triangle.");
        }
    }
    class Rectangle : Shape
    {
        public override void AboutMe()
        {
            Console.WriteLine("It is a Rectangle");
        }
    }
```

Now assume that a new class named GrandShape derives from both Triangle and Rectangle. Figure 2-3 shows a sample class diagram for this.

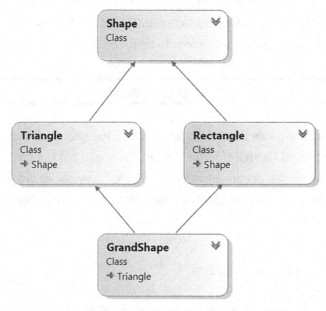

Figure 2-3. *Diamond problem due to multiple inheritance*

Now we have an ambiguity. From which class will GrandShape inherit or call AboutMe()? Is it from Triangle, or is it from Rectangle? To remove this type of ambiguity, C# does not support the concept of multiple inheritance through the class. This problem is known as the *Diamond problem*. So, if you code like this:

```
// Error due to the Diamond Effect
class GrandShape: Triangle, Rectangle
 {
      // Some  code
 }
```

you will notice that the C# compiler shows you the following error:

```
CS1721 Class 'GrandShape' cannot have multiple base classes: 'Triangle' and
'Rectangle'
```

You can see that C# designers wanted to avoid any unwanted outcome in an application because of this kind of support. Their key goal was to make the language simple and less error-prone. When you support special scenarios like this, you need to implement additional rules to validate them. Maintaining this kind of additional rule can make a programming language complex. But yes, in the end, it is up to the team that designs the language.

Initial Program

Let us consider some vehicles that can either float or fly. Since boats float and airplanes fly, I use a Boat class and an Airplane class in the upcoming example. Similar to the demonstrations in the previous chapter, I'll show you some code segments which we'll improve later. Let's look into the following demonstration now.

Demonstration 1

In this example, there are two different types of vehicles. So, you can start with the interface IVehicle to form the following inheritance hierarchy:

```
interface IVehicle
{
    void Fly();
    void Float();
}
class Boat: IVehicle
{
    public void Float()
```

```
    {
        Console.WriteLine("It will float now.");
    }

    public void Fly()
    {
        throw new NotImplementedException();
    }
}
class Airplane: IVehicle
{
    public void Float()
    {
        throw new NotImplementedException();
    }

    public void Fly()
    {
        Console.WriteLine("It will fly now.");
    }
}
```

But you may prefer an abstract class over an interface. So, you can redesign the code as follows:

```
abstract class Vehicle
{
    public abstract void Float();
    public abstract void Fly();
}
class Boat : Vehicle
{
    public override void Float()
    {
        Console.WriteLine("It will float now.");
    }
    public override void Fly()
```

CHAPTER 2   ABSTRACT CLASS OR INTERFACE?

```csharp
        {
            throw new NotImplementedException();
        }
    }
    class Airplane : Vehicle
    {
        public override void Float()
        {
            throw new NotImplementedException();
        }

        public override void Fly()
        {
            Console.WriteLine("It will fly now.");
        }
    }
```

At this point, these two designs may appear to be the same. Now let's say you need to consider a new type of vehicle: ship. You know that if you consider only the vehicles that either float or fly, you can put a common behavior inside the abstract class. In our case, out of these three types of vehicles, ships and boats float, but they do not fly. So, it may appear that you can make a common Float() method and move it to the abstract class. Then you remove the Fly() method from the Boat and Ship classes. This is reasonable too. If you do this, the Boat and Ship classes can use the base class's Float() method without overriding this method inside them. (Obviously, they can override the behavior if they want.)

Consider airplanes now. You cannot remove the Fly() method from the Airplane class. So, if you need to add a new type of vehicle with different behaviors, the maintenance of the code becomes tough. When you have a ship, boat, and airplane, you may find that placing the Float() method in an abstract class is beneficial. But if you have a ship, boat, airplane, helicopter, and rocket, you find that the Fly() method in the abstract class is more beneficial for you. So, it may not always be easy to determine which behaviors you should consider as common behavior (particularly in a growing application that keeps adding different vehicles).

It is not the only issue to consider. Later you'll see the SOLID principles (Chapter 4), and you will learn that it is not a good idea to put many different behaviors in a single class even if this design may seem to be appealing when you have so many common behaviors among many different classes.

27

Now go back to the initial code segment where you considered only boats and airplanes. In this case, if you use an interface, you need to implement all the interface methods. As a result, since boats do not fly, you needed to override the `Fly()` method in the `Boat` class as follows:

```
public void Fly()
{
    throw new NotImplementedException();
}
```

Again, airplanes do not float in normal situations. So, you needed to override the method as follows:

```
public void Float()
{
    throw new NotImplementedException();
}
```

This kind of code creates a problem when you try to use polymorphic code. As per these implementations, they can throw exceptions when you iterate over the vehicles using supertype references and try to access the fly or float behaviors. For example, the following code segment raises an exception:

```
List<IVehicle> vehicles = new()
 {
  new Boat(),
  new Airplane()
 };
// Following code will raise an exception
foreach (IVehicle vehicle in vehicles)
{
    vehicle.Float();
    vehicle.Fly();
}
```

Note   In Chapter 4, when I discuss the Liskov substitution principle (LSP), you'll see a detailed discussion about this.

In addition to the issues mentioned, consider some unusual situations such as an airplane needing to float to survive an exceptional situation. Or consider technological enhancements; we might expect to see flying cars. These considerations give you a clue that separating behavior from a vehicle can help you maintain the application easily. So, instead of writing a complete program that follows the initial design, let us jump to the next section where you start with a better approach.

Better Program

Suppose each vehicle should have a registration number from the government of the country. In this case, you're likely to use this field inside an abstract class. But if you need to consider the different types of vehicles such as airplanes, ships, or boats that can show different behaviors, an interface is a better choice. What can you do now? Your guess is correct. You can combine an abstract class with an interface in your application. As discussed, this time you separate the vehicle behavior and form a different inheritance hierarchy. This kind of design helps you to add dynamic behavior to a vehicle. Follow along with the second demonstration.

Demonstration 2

In this demonstration, you see two different inheritance hierarchies. Here are the important considerations:

- All the vehicle behaviors form one hierarchy. I assume that, initially, a vehicle cannot do anything special. To represent this, I add a DoNothing behavior in the born state. In some later stages, you can add the float or fly capability to a vehicle. To represent these two behaviors, I use the FloatCapability and FlyCapability classes, respectively. So, I have an inheritance hierarchy where you see an interface ICapability with three different classes: FloatCapability, FlyCapability, and DoNothing.

Figure 2-4 shows this inheritance chain.

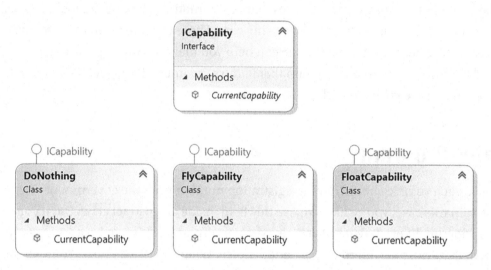

Figure 2-4. *All the possible vehicle behaviors form one inheritance hierarchy*

The following code segment represents this inheritance chain, which I put in a separate namespace:

```
namespace Capabilities
{
    interface ICapability
    {
        void CurrentCapability();
    }
    class FloatCapability : ICapability
    {
        public void CurrentCapability()
        {
            Console.WriteLine("It will float now.");
        }
    }
    class FlyCapability : ICapability
    {
        public void CurrentCapability()
        {
```

```
        Console.WriteLine("It will fly now.");
    }
}
class DoNothing : ICapability
{
    public void CurrentCapability()
    {
        Console.WriteLine("It does nothing.");
    }
}
}
```

I place the different vehicles in a separate inheritance hierarchy. This time I start with an abstract class called Vehicle. The Boat and Airplane classes derive from this class. Here are the additional considerations:

- I assume each vehicle has a registration number, and a vehicle can show one behavior at a particular time. But you can change the behavior if you want.

- To set a particular behavior (or, capability), I use the SetVehicleBehavior() method. To show the current details of a vehicle, there is a DisplayDetails() method.

- I place these methods and fields in the abstract class Vehicle, which is as follows:

```
abstract class Vehicle
{
    protected string vehicleType = string.Empty;
    protected ICapability capability;
    protected string registrationNumber = string.Empty;
    public abstract void SetVehicleBehavior(ICapability capability);
    public abstract void DisplayDetails();
}
```

Note   You can see that the SetVehicleBehavior(...) method accepts a polymorphic argument, which is nothing but a vehicle behavior. I highlight it in bold.

- I mentioned earlier that in the born state a vehicle does not have any special behavior. So, I add the DoNothing behavior to it in the born state. To illustrate this, here is a sample code for you from the Boat class constructor:

```
public Boat(string registrationId)
{
    registrationNumber = registrationId;
    vehicleType = "Boat";
    capability = new DoNothing();
}
```

Figure 2-5 summarizes the details.

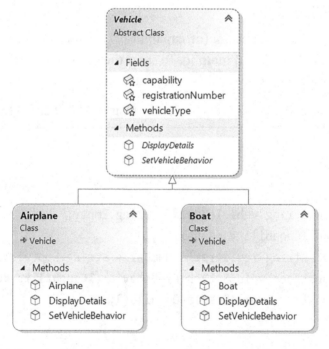

Figure 2-5.   *Vehicle, Airplane, and Boat form an inheritance hierarchy*

POINT TO REMEMBER

If by mistake you place the instance fields `vehicleType`, `capability`, and `registrationNumber` in an interface, you receive the compile-time error CS 0525 saying: `Interfaces cannot contain instance fields`.

So, if you want to use instance fields, you need an abstract class.

For simplicity, I have put everything in a single file. Now go through the complete implementation and output, shown here:

```
using Vehicles;
using Capabilities;
try
{
    Console.WriteLine("***Vehicles with different capabilities demo.***");
    Console.WriteLine("Using a boat.");
    Vehicle vehicle = new Boat("B001");
    vehicle.DisplayDetails();
    Console.WriteLine("***************");

    ICapability currentCapability = new FloatCapability();
    Console.WriteLine("Setting floating capability.");
    vehicle.SetVehicleBehavior(currentCapability);
    vehicle.DisplayDetails();
    Console.WriteLine("***************");

    Console.WriteLine("Using an airplane.");
    vehicle = new Airplane("A002");
    Console.WriteLine("Setting flying capability.");
    currentCapability = new FlyCapability();
    vehicle.SetVehicleBehavior(currentCapability);
    vehicle.DisplayDetails();
    Console.WriteLine("***************");
```

```
        Console.WriteLine("Adding floating behavior to it.");
        currentCapability = new FloatCapability();
        vehicle.SetVehicleBehavior(currentCapability);
        vehicle.DisplayDetails();
        Console.WriteLine("***************");
}
catch (Exception ex)
{
        Console.WriteLine($"Error:{ex}");
}
namespace Capabilities
{
        interface ICapability
        {
            void CurrentCapability();
        }
        class FloatCapability : ICapability
        {
            public void CurrentCapability()
            {
                Console.WriteLine("It will float now.");
            }
        }
        class FlyCapability : ICapability
        {
            public void CurrentCapability()
            {
                Console.WriteLine("It will fly now.");
            }
        }
        class DoNothing : ICapability
        {
            public void CurrentCapability()
            {
```

```csharp
            Console.WriteLine("It does nothing.");
        }
    }
}

namespace Vehicles
{
    abstract class Vehicle
    {
        protected string vehicleType = string.Empty;
        protected ICapability capability;
        protected string registrationNumber = string.Empty;
        public abstract void SetVehicleBehavior(ICapability capability);
        public abstract void DisplayDetails();
    }

    class Boat : Vehicle
    {
        public Boat(string registrationId)
        {
            registrationNumber = registrationId;
            vehicleType = "Boat";
            capability = new DoNothing();
        }
        public override void SetVehicleBehavior(ICapability capability)
        {
            this.capability = capability;
        }
        public override void DisplayDetails()
        {
            Console.WriteLine("**The current status of the boat**");
            Console.WriteLine($"Registration number: {registrationNumber}");
            capability.CurrentCapability();
        }
    }
```

```csharp
    class Airplane : Vehicle
    {
        public Airplane(string registrationId)
        {
            registrationNumber = registrationId;
            vehicleType = "Airplane";
            capability = new DoNothing();
        }
        public override void SetVehicleBehavior(ICapability capability)
        {
            this.capability = capability;
        }
        public override void DisplayDetails()
        {
            Console.WriteLine("**The current status of the airplane**");
            Console.WriteLine($"Registration number: {registrationNumber}");
            capability.CurrentCapability();
        }
    }
}
```

Output

Here is the output:

```
***Vehicles with different capabilities demo.***
Using a boat.
**The current status of the boat**
Registration number:B001
It does nothing.
***************
Setting floating capability.
**The current status of the boat**
Registration number:B001
It will float now.
***************
```

```
Using an airplane.
Setting flying capability.
**The current status of the airplane**
Registration number: A002
It will fly now.
***************
Adding floating behavior to it.
**The current status of the airplane**
Registration number: A002
It will float now.
***************
```

Analysis

The competitor to inheritance is composition. When you use object composition, you do a HAS-A test. You can relate this with real-world examples. For example, we say that the car HAS-A beautiful body, or the human body HAS A brain that it uses. In programming, suppose you represent the human body with a class called HUMAN and a human brain with a class BRAIN. Now to represent the line "A human uses its brain," you create a BRAIN reference (instead of reference, developers often use the term 'reference variable', or simply a variable) inside the HUMAN class.

Have you noticed that in our code example, each vehicle has different behaviors that it uses? How did we represent these behaviors? You know that there is a separate inheritance chain and all these behaviors are implemented in the ICapability interface. Notice that the Vehicle class contains an ICapability reference. It helps a vehicle to show the correct behavior in a particular moment. You also noticed that each vehicle can change its behavior at runtime too. To achieve these functionalities, you needed to ensure that each behavior implements the behavior interface properly.

This example shows that by combining the real power of an abstract class, interfaces, and object composition, you can write an efficient application.

Summary

This chapter compared the uses of an abstract class over an interface and vice versa. Note that there are also scenarios where you are bound to use only one of them. For example, an interface does not include instance data such as fields, auto-implemented properties, or property-like events. On the contrary, if you want to simulate inheritance for structs, the interface is your only option. This is because they cannot inherit from another struct or class.

This chapter investigated the situations where you can opt for either an abstract class or an interface. We also analyzed the consequence of the choice. In short, if you want to have a centralized behavior, use an abstract class. But when you want the class-specific implementations, use an interface. This chapter answered the following questions:

- When is an abstract class a better choice over an interface?

- When is an interface a better choice over an abstract class?

- What is a diamond problem?

- How can you do a HAS-A test?

- How can object composition offer a better solution?

- How can you change an object's behavior at runtime?

- How can you combine an abstract class with an interface to make an efficient application?

CHAPTER 3

Wise Use of Code Comments

Comments help you understand other people's codes. They can describe the logic behind the code. But expert programmers are particular about comments and do not like to see unnecessary comments. This chapter provides case studies to help you decide whether to put a comment in your application.

Recap of Code Comments

It is a standard practice to use comments in your program. The C# compiler ignores the comments, but they can help others to understand your code better. Let us consider a real-life scenario. In a software organization, say a group of people are creating software for its customers. It is possible that after some years, none of these people work at the organization anymore. In such a case, someone needs to maintain the software and continue fixing the bugs for its customers. But it is difficult to understand a complex working mechanism if there is no explanation of the program's logic. Comments are useful in such scenarios. These help us understand the code better.

In C#, you see the following type of comments:

Type 1: Single-line comments use a double forward slash (//). Here is a code segment that starts with a single-line comment:

```
// Testing whether 2 is greater than 1
Console.WriteLine(2 > 1);
```

Type 2: You can use multiline comments to comment on more than one line at a time. You use this to comment out a block of statements. Here is a code segment that starts with multiline comments:

© Vaskaran Sarcar 2023
V. Sarcar, *Simple and Efficient Programming with C#*, https://doi.org/10.1007/978-1-4842-8737-8_3

```
/*
Now I use multi-line comments.
It spans multiple lines.
Here I multiply 2 by 3.
*/
Console.WriteLine(2 * 3);
```

Type 3: Documentation comments are special comments. You can create documentation for your code using this type of comment that contains XML text. There are two types: either they start with three slashes (///), often called single-line documentation comments, or they are delimited comments that start with a slash and two stars (/**). Here is a code segment that uses single-line documentation comments:

```
/// <summary>
/// <para>This is a custom class.</para>
/// <br>There is no method inside it.</br>
/// </summary>
class Sample
{

}
```

Here is a code segment that uses a different form:

```
/**
 * <summary>
 * <para>This is another custom class.</para>
 * <br>It is also empty now.</br>
 * </summary>
 */
class AnotherSample
{

}
```

In the end, the key aim is the same: comments help others to understand why you write a piece of code.

POINTS IN A NUTSHELL

- Comments are simple notes or some text. You use them for human readers, not for the C# compiler. The C# compiler ignores the text inside a comment block.

- In the software industry, many technical reviewers review your code. The comments help them understand the program's logic.

- Developers can forget how the complex logic works after several months too. These comments can help them remember what the code does.

Initial Program

You know that when the C# compiler sees a comment, it ignores it. In demonstration 1, you can see a complete program with many different comments. Compile and run this program to ensure you see the expected output.

Demonstration 1

In this program, you calculate the area of a rectangle. Here is the complete demonstration:

```
Console.WriteLine("***Measuring the area of a rectangle.***");
Rectangle r = new (2.5, 10);
double area = r.Area();
Console.WriteLine($"The area of the rectangle is {area} square units.");

/// <summary>
/// This is the Rectangle class
/// </summary>
class Rectangle
{
    readonly double l; // length of the rectangle
    readonly double b; // breadth of the rectangle
    public Rectangle(double le, double br)
```

```
    {
        l = le;
        b = br;
    }
    // Measuring the area
    public double Area()
    {
        return l * b;
    }
}
```

Output

Here is the output:

```
***Measuring the area of a rectangle.***
The area of the rectangle is 25 square units.
```

Analysis

This program uses different types of comments to explain the code. These are not doing any harm to the program. Now the question is, are they necessary? You will find many people in the software industry who dislike comments. They believe that people without a programming background do not read your code, which is true. Normally, a programmer or a developer is the only one who reads your code. No one likes to read an unnecessary explanation if the code is easily understandable. Also, older comments can be misleading if you do not maintain them. My belief is that comments are good if they are necessary. I dislike unnecessary comments, and I like to remove them if my code is expressive enough.

Better Program

Can you rewrite the program in demonstration 1 without comments? Yes, you can. You can delete all these comments at any time. Then you compile and run the program to confirm the same output. But the question is: when you do that, will your code be readable? Can a person understand it easily? Let's take a look at demonstration 2.

Demonstration 2

Here is demonstration 2. It is a modified version of demonstration 1 and produces the same output. What are the changes? Notice that I have renamed the variables and the area method inside the Rectangle class. These new names are expressive enough. Anyone who reads this code should have a better idea about what I'm trying to do.

```
Console.WriteLine("***Measuring the area of a rectangle.***");
Rectangle rectangleObject = new(2.5, 10);
double area = rectangleObject.RectangleArea();
Console.WriteLine($"The area of the rectangle is {area} square units.");

class Rectangle
{
    readonly double length;
    readonly double breadth;
    public Rectangle(double length, double breadth)
    {
        this.length = length;
        this.breadth = breadth;
    }

    public double RectangleArea()
    {
        return length * breadth;
    }
}
```

Analysis

This demonstration is easy to understand. Did you notice that this time I chose variable names such as length and breadth? But in demonstration 1, I used an l (a lowercase L, not 1) and b, respectively. To let others understand this code, I needed to write the inline comments such as // length of the rectangle or // breadth of the rectangle. In this context, though it is easy to read, this type of comment can create confusion if you read this code on a device that has a smaller display.

Microsoft (see `https://docs.microsoft.com/en-us/dotnet/csharp/fundamentals/coding-style/coding-conventions`) also recommends not putting a comment at the end of a line. It suggests putting a comment always on a separate line.

But, when you choose a method name such as `RectangleArea()`,one can presume what this method is about to do, and as a result, you do not need to write additional comments for it. A similar type of method name is useful if you work on areas of different shapes such as circles, squares, or triangles.

POINTS TO REMEMBER

Here are Microsoft's guidelines for the proper use of comments. In practice, we often violate this in a demo application, but these suggestions are helpful when you write enterprise code:

- Begin comments with an uppercase letter and end with a period.

- Place comments on a separate line, instead of putting them at the end of lines of code.

- There should be a space between the comment delimiter (`//`) and the comment text. Here is a sample:

  ```
  // This is a sample comment.
  ```

- Avoid creating formatted blocks of asterisks around comments.

- You need to assure that the public members have the necessary XML comments to describe their behavior. (I admit that I am often lazy about this, particularly when the behaviors of a type are simple and easy to understand.)

Use the Power of C#

Sometimes you see some comments that appear very helpful at the beginning. The following code shows a TODO comment saying that you do not intend to use the SayHello() method in the future. It suggests using the SayHi method starting with the next release.

```
class Sample
{
    readonly string name = "Reader";
```

```csharp
// TODO-We'll replace this method shortly.
// Use SayHi() from the next release(Version-2.0).

public void SayHello()
{
    Console.WriteLine($"Hello, {name}!");
}

public void SayHi()
{
    Console.WriteLine($"\nHi, {name}!");
    Console.WriteLine("This is the latest method.");
}
}
```

This TODO comment seems to be easy to understand and useful. Now see some sample client code that uses these methods:

```csharp
Console.WriteLine("Dealing with TODO comments.");
Sample sample = new ();
sample.SayHello();
sample.SayHi();
```

This client code is also simple. There is nothing special in this code. Think about it from a company perspective now. A company does not share the actual code with its clients. Instead, the company tells the client how to use the functionalities of the application. But how will the client know that he needs to use SayHi() starting with version 2.0? One way is to include this information in the user manual. But there is an alternative approach too. You can use the power of attributes. This is better in the sense that human behavior often resists the changes. If they can do the work using an old method, it is very much likely that they are too lazy to test the new method. So, I'll show you a better alternative now. Notice the Sample class that uses an attribute, called Obsolete, to indicate that SayHello() should not be used in the upcoming development work.

Demonstration 3

Here is the complete program:

```
Console.WriteLine("Dealing with TODO comments.");
Sample sample = new ();
sample.SayHello();
sample.SayHi();
class Sample
{
    readonly string name = "Reader";
    [Obsolete("This method is obsolete. Use SayHi() instead.")]
    public void SayHello()
    {
        Console.WriteLine($"Hello, {name}!");
    }

    public void SayHi()
    {
        Console.WriteLine($"Hi, {name}!");
        Console.WriteLine("This is the latest method.");
    }
}
```

Analysis

Now the same client code will notice that the SayHello() method is obsolete. The clients also get the information that they should use SayHi() instead of this old method. Figure 3-1 shows a snapshot of the Visual Studio IDE, which gives you the idea.

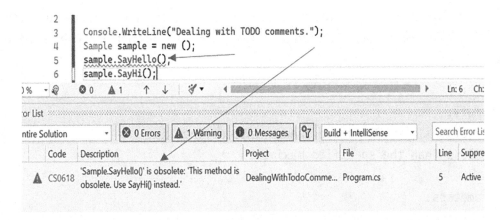

Figure 3-1. *The SayHello() method is obsolete*

Summary

The book *Clean Code* (Pearson) by Robert C. Martin tells us the following: "Comments are always failures. We must have them because we cannot always figure out how to express ourselves without them, but their use is not a cause for celebration." This book continues, "Every time you express yourself in code, you should pat yourself on the back. Every time you write a comment, you should grimace and feel the failure of your ability of expression." Another great book is *The Pragmatic Programmer* by Andrew Hunt and David Thomas that tells us: "Programmers are taught to comment their code: good code has lots of comments. Unfortunately, they are never taught why code needs comments: bad code requires lots of comments."

You may not always agree with these thoughts, but you will find people who can point to pros and cons on both sides of the issue. Even these books show some examples of both good and bad comments.

There are plenty of examples where the actual code is tricky or difficult to understand. Some good, well-maintained comments can help a first-time reader/ developer. For me, when I hover my mouse over a built-in function, a comment helps me to understand the method better. In this book, I have generated some random numbers in many examples. There are overloaded methods to do this activity. For example, I often use the following form:

```
// The previous code is skipped
Random r = new();
r.Next(12);
```

The associated comments are straightforward for me to understand how this method works. The following built-in comments are associated with this particular version of the Next method:

```
//
// Summary:
//      Returns a non-negative random integer that is
//      less than the specified maximum.
//
// Parameters:
//    maxValue:
//      The exclusive upper bound of the random number
//      to be generated. maxValue must
//      be greater than or equal to 0.
//
// Returns:
//      A 32-bit signed integer that is greater than or
//      equal to 0, and less than maxValue;
//      that is, the range of return values ordinarily
//      includes 0 but not maxValue. However,
//      if maxValue equals 0, maxValue is returned.
//
// Exceptions:
//    T:System.ArgumentOutOfRangeException:
//      maxValue is less than 0.
public virtual int Next(int maxValue);
```

This is the reason I suggest you stop and think before you place a comment in your code. Use them when they are truly beneficial. You can get a better idea of this when your code goes through peer reviews.

Note   This is nothing worse than a line of commented code that references a method or variables that are no longer in use. It can also cause trouble when you use a comment that does not stay close to the actual code. You may even see comments that give you incorrect information. At any cost, you should not allow bad or unnecessary comments to remain in your application.

Finally, comments are not always used to describe the code. You may see commented-out code in an application too. Keeping commented-out code is not a recommended practice; however, I use some commented-out code in my books for further demonstration purposes. For example, I may point out an alternative way of calling a method. Sometimes I keep the commented-out code with potential output to show you correct or incorrect behavior. But following the experts' suggestion, I do not like to see unnecessary commented code in an enterprise application. This is because, if needed, you can always track down the old code from a source code version management tool such as Git or SVN.

In short, this chapter discussed the following questions:

- What are code comments?

- What are the different types of comments?

- Why are good comments beneficial?

- Why are unnecessary comments bad, and how can you avoid them?

- How can you avoid specific plain comments using C# language features?

PART II

Important Principles

Part II consists of two chapters, in which we'll examine the use of the following:

- SOLID principles. These are a combination of five design guidelines.

- Don't repeat yourself (DRY) principle.

In an object-oriented programming world, there is no shortage of principles, but those we will discuss in the next two chapters are the fundamental design guidelines for a better application. One cannot predict all future requirements in advance, so changes are often needed in enterprise applications. This is why a flexible application that can adopt future requirements easily is considered a better application. This part will review case studies using (and not using) these principles and help you think about their importance. A detailed study of these principles can help you create efficient applications.

CHAPTER 4

Know SOLID Principles

C# is a powerful language. It supports object-oriented programming and has lots of features. I believe that compared to the old days, coding is easier with the support of these powerful features. But the hard truth is that simply using these features in an application does not guarantee that you have used them in the right way. In any given requirement, it is vital to identify the purpose of classes, objects, and how they communicate with each other. In addition, your application must be flexible and extendable to fulfill future enhancements. Now the question is, where are these guidelines? To answer this, you need to follow experts' footprints. Robert C. Martin is a famous name in the programming world. He is an American software engineer, is a best-selling author, and is also known as Uncle Bob. He has promoted many principles, and a subset of them are as follows:

- **S**ingle Responsibility Principle (SRP)

- **O**pen/Closed Principle (OCP)

- **L**iskov Substitution Principle (LSP)

- **I**nterface Segregation Principle (ISP)

- **D**ependency Inversion Principle (DIP)

Robert C. Martin and Micah Martin also discussed these principles in their book *Agile Principles, Patterns, and Practices in C#* (Prentice Hall). Taking the first letter of each principle, Michael Feathers introduced the SOLID acronym so we can remember these names easily.

Before you read further, I remind you that these design principles are some high-level guidelines that you can use to make better software. They are not bound to any particular computer language. So, if you understand these concepts using C#, you can use them with similar languages like Java or C++. See `https://sites.google.com/site/unclebobconsultingllc/getting-a-solid-start` to learn more about Robert C. Martin's ideas.

© Vaskaran Sarcar 2023
V. Sarcar, *Simple and Efficient Programming with C#*, https://doi.org/10.1007/978-1-4842-8737-8_4

The SOLID principles are not rules. They are not laws. They are not perfect truths. They are statements on the order of "An apple a day keeps the doctor away." This is a good principle, it is good advice, but it's not a pure truth, nor is it a rule.

—Robert C. Martin

In this chapter, we'll explore these principles in detail. One way to understand a principle is to recognize its need in the first place. So, in each case, I start with a program that does not follow any specific design guidelines but compiles and runs successfully. Then in the "Analysis" section, we'll discuss the possible drawbacks and try to find a better solution using these principles. These case studies will help you think better and make high-quality applications.

Single Responsibility Principle

A class acts like a container that can hold many things such as data, properties, or methods. If you put too much data, properties, or methods together that are not related to each other, you end up with a bulky class that can create problems in the future. Let us consider an example. Suppose you create a class with multiple methods that do different things. In such a case, even if you make a small change in one method, you need to retest the whole class again to ensure the workflow is correct. This is because changes in one method can impact the other methods in the class. This is the reason that the single responsibility principle opposes the idea of putting multiple responsibilities in a class. It says that ***a class should have only one reason to change.***

Note   To describe the principle, I used the concept of a class. Robert C. Martin described this principle in terms of modules. The term *module* can be confusing for you if you purely think in terms of C#. For example, the Microsoft documentation (see `https://docs.microsoft.com/en-us/dotnet/api/system.reflection.module?view=net-6.0`) says the following: "A module is a portable executable file, such as type .dll or application .exe, consisting of one or more classes and interfaces. There may be multiple namespaces contained in a single module, and a namespace may span multiple modules." This documentation also says that a .NET Framework module is not the same as a module in Visual

Basic, which is used by programmers to organize functions and subroutines in an application. Similarly, any Python programmer knows that a module can contain many things. To organize his code, a Python programmer can place variables, functions, and classes in a module. The programmer creates a separate file with a .py extension for this purpose. Later the programmer can import the whole module or a particular function from the module in the current file.

To make things easy, I'll use classes to describe this principle and subsequent principles in this chapter.

So, before you make a class, identify the responsibility or the purpose of the class. If multiple members help you to achieve one single purpose, you can place all the members inside the class.

POINTS TO REMEMBER

When you follow the SRP, your code is smaller, cleaner, and less fragile. Now the question is, how do you follow this principle? A simple answer is that you can divide a big problem into smaller chunks based on different responsibilities and put each of these small parts into separate classes. The next question is, what do we mean by responsibility? In simple words, *responsibility is a reason for a change*.

Let us consider some examples. For an Employee class, suppose you see methods such as SaveEmpDetails(Employee e), DisplaySalary(Employee e), etc. Probably, you can guess that SaveEmpDetails will save the details of an employee to a database. So, a database administrator should be responsible for ensuring everything is maintained properly. You can also guess that DisplaySalary will probably show the salary details of an employee. Now the question is, who maintains them? Probably the account head of the company will be responsible for ensuring that it shows the correct data. So, you can see that different people are "responsible" for changes.

In the upcoming discussion, you'll see a class that contains three different methods that are not closely related to each other. We'll analyze the impact, and in the end, I'll segregate the code based on different responsibilities and put them into different classes. Let's start.

Initial Program

In demonstration 1, you see an Employee class with three different methods. Here are the details:

- The DisplayEmployeeDetail() method shows the employee's name and his working experience in years.

- The CheckSeniority() method can evaluate whether an employee is a senior person. To make things simple, I assume that if the employee has 5+ years of experience, they are a senior employee; otherwise, they are a junior employee.

- The GenerateEmployeeId() method generates an employee ID using string concatenation. The logic is simple: I concatenate the first letter of the first name with a random number to form an employee ID. In the client code, I'll create two Employee instances and use these methods to display the relevant details.

Demonstration 1

Here is the complete demonstration:

```
Console.WriteLine("*** A demo without SRP.***");
Employee robin = new("Robin", "Smith", 7.5);
robin.DisplayEmployeeDetail();
string empId = robin.GenerateEmployeeId(robin.FirstName);
Console.WriteLine($"The employee id: {empId}");

Console.WriteLine($"This employee is a " +
  $"{robin.CheckSeniority(robin.ExperienceInYears)}
  employee.");

Console.WriteLine("*******");

Employee kevin = new("Kevin", "Proctor", 3.2);
kevin.DisplayEmployeeDetail();
empId = kevin.GenerateEmployeeId(kevin.FirstName);
Console.WriteLine($"The employee id: {empId}");
Console.WriteLine($"This employee is a " +
```

```
  $"{kevin.CheckSeniority(kevin.ExperienceInYears)}
  employee.");

class Employee
{
    public string FirstName, LastName;
    public string Id;
    public double ExperienceInYears;
    public Employee(
        string firstName,
        string lastName,
        double experience)
    {
        FirstName = firstName;
        LastName = lastName;
        ExperienceInYears = experience;
        Id = "Not generated yet";
    }
    public void DisplayEmployeeDetail()
    {
        Console.WriteLine($"The employee name:
         {LastName}, {FirstName}");
        Console.WriteLine($"This employee has
         {ExperienceInYears} years of experience.");
    }

    public string CheckSeniority(double experienceInYears)
    {
        if (experienceInYears > 5)
            return "senior";
        else
            return "junior";
    }
    public string GenerateEmployeeId(string empFirstName)
    {
```

```
        int random = new Random().Next(1000);
        Id = string.Concat(empFirstName[0], random);
        return Id;
    }
}
```

Output

Here is some sample output (the employee ID can vary in your case):

```
*** A demo without SRP.***
The employee name: Smith, Robin
This employee has 7.5 years of experience.
The employee id: R531
This employee is a senior employee.
*******
The employee name: Proctor, Kevin
This employee has 3.2 years of experience.
The employee id: K609
This employee is a junior employee.
```

Analysis

What is the problem with this design? This answer is that I violate the SRP here. You can see that displaying an employee detail, generating an employee ID, and checking a seniority level all are different activities. You also understand that different people are responsible for maintaining this data properly. Since I put everything in a single class, I may face problems adopting new changes in the future. Here are some possible reasons:

- The top management can set different criteria to decide on a seniority level.

- The human resource department can use a new algorithm to generate the employee ID.

In each case, you need to modify the Employee class and so forth. You understand that it is better to follow the SRP and separate the activities.

Better Program

In the following demonstration, I introduce two more classes. The SeniorityChecker class now contains the CheckSeniority() method, and the EmployeeIdGenerator class contains the GenerateEmployeeId() method to generate the employee ID. As a result, in the future, if you need to change the program logic to determine the seniority level or use a new algorithm to generate an employee ID, you can make the changes in the respective classes. Other classes are untouched. So, you do not need to retest those classes. Now you have followed the SRP.

In addition, apart from following the SRP, this time I improved the code readability too. Notice that in demonstration 1, I called all the required methods inside the client code. But for better readability and to avoid clumsiness, this time I introduce three static methods: PrintEmployeeDetail(...), PrintEmployeeId(...), and PrintSeniorityLevel(...). I have defined them inside a helper class, called Helper. These methods call the DisplayEmployeeDetail() method from Employee, the GenerateEmployeeId() method from EmployeeIdGenerator, and the CheckSeniority() method from SeniorityChecker, respectively. I repeat that these three methods are not necessary, but they make the client code simple and easily understandable.

Demonstration 2

Here is the complete demonstration that follows the SRP:

```
Console.WriteLine("*** A demo that follows SRP.***");

Employee robin = new("Robin", "Smith", 7.5);

Helper.PrintEmployeeDetail(robin);
Helper.PrintEmployeeId(robin);
Helper.PrintSeniorityLevel(robin);

Console.WriteLine("*******");

Employee kevin = new("Kevin", "Proctor", 3.2);

Helper.PrintEmployeeDetail(kevin);
Helper.PrintEmployeeId(kevin);
Helper.PrintSeniorityLevel(kevin);
```

```
class Employee
{
    public string FirstName, LastName;
    public double ExperienceInYears;
    public Employee(
        string firstName,
        string lastName,
        double experience)
    {
        FirstName = firstName;
        LastName = lastName;
        ExperienceInYears = experience;
    }

    public void DisplayEmployeeDetail()
    {
        Console.WriteLine($"The employee name:
         {LastName}, {FirstName}");
        Console.WriteLine($"This employee has
        {ExperienceInYears} years of experience.");
    }
}
class SeniorityChecker
{
    public string CheckSeniority(
     double experienceInYears)
    {
        if (experienceInYears > 5)
            return "senior";
        else
            return "junior";
    }

}
```

```
class EmployeeIdGenerator
{
    public string Id = "Not generated yet";
    public string GenerateEmployeeId(string
     empFirstName)
    {
        int random = new Random().Next(1000);
        Id = string.Concat(empFirstName[0], random);
        return Id;
    }
}
class Helper
{
    public static void PrintEmployeeDetail(Employee emp)
    {
        emp.DisplayEmployeeDetail();
    }

    public static void PrintEmployeeId(Employee emp)
    {
      EmployeeIdGenerator idGenerator = new();
      string empId =
       idGenerator.GenerateEmployeeId(emp.FirstName);
      Console.WriteLine($"The employee id: {empId}");
    }
    public static void PrintSeniorityLevel(Employee emp)
    {
        SeniorityChecker seniorityChecker = new();
        string seniorityLevel =
         seniorityChecker.CheckSeniority(
          emp.ExperienceInYears);
        Console.WriteLine($"This employee is a
         {seniorityLevel} employee.");
    }
}
```

Output

Here is some possible output. Notice that it is similar to the previous output, except the first line that says that this program follows the SRP now. I said before that the employee ID can vary in your case.

```
*** A demo that follows SRP.***
The employee name: Smith, Robin
This employee has 7.5 years of experience.
The employee id: R46
This employee is a senior employee.
*******
The employee name: Proctor, Kevin
This employee has 3.2 years of experience.
The employee id: K261
This employee is a junior employee.
```

POINT TO NOTE

Note that the SRP does not say that a class should have at most one method. Here the emphasis is on the single responsibility. There may be closely related methods that can help you to implement a responsibility. For example, if you have different methods to display the first name, the last name, and a full name, you can put these methods in the same class. These methods are closely related, and it makes sense to place all these display methods inside the same class.

In addition, you should not conclude that you need to separate responsibilities in every application that you make. You must analyze the change's nature. This is because too many classes can make your application complex, which is difficult to maintain. But if you know this principle and think carefully before you implement a design, you are likely to avoid similar mistakes that I discussed earlier.

Open/Closed Principle

According to Robert C. Martin, the OCP is the most important principle among all the principles of object-oriented design. In the book *Clean Architecture* (Pearson), he says the following:

> The Open-Closed Principle(OCP) was coined in 1988 by Bertrand Meyer. It says: **A software artifact should be open for extension but closed for modification.**

In this section, we'll examine the OCP principle in detail using custom classes in C#. Once I went through *Object-Oriented Software Construction* (Second Edition) by Bertrand Meyer, I understood some important thoughts behind this principle. Let me pick some of them:

- Any modular decomposition technique must satisfy the OCP: modules should be both open and closed.

- The contradiction between the two terms is apparent because they have different goals:

  - A module is said to be open if it is still available for extension. For example, it should be possible to expand its set of operations or add fields to its data structures.

  - A module is said to be closed if it is available for use by other modules. This assumes that the module has been given a well-defined, stable description (its interface in the sense of information hiding). At the implementation level, closure for a module also implies that you may compile it, perhaps store it in a library, and make it available for others (its clients) to use.

- The need for modules to be closed and the need for them to remain open arise for different reasons.

- He explains that openness is useful for software developers because they can't foresee all the elements that a module may need in the future. But the "closed" modules will satisfy the need of the project managers because they want to complete the project instead of waiting for each other to complete their parts.

The previous points are self-explanatory. You understand that the idea behind this design philosophy is that in a stable and working application, once you create a class and other parts of your application start using it, any further change in the class can cause the working application to break. If you require new features (or, functionalities), instead of changing the existing class, you can extend the class to adopt those new requirements. What is the benefit? Since you do not change the old code, your existing functionalities continue to work without any problem, and you can avoid testing them again. Instead, you need to test the "extended" part (or, functionalities) only.

In 1988, Bertrand Meyer suggested the use of inheritance in this context. He says the following:

> *A class is closed, since it may be compiled, stored in a library, baselined, and used by client classes. But it is also open, since any new class may use it as a parent, adding new features and redeclaring inherited features; in this process there is no need to change the original or to disturb its clients. This property is fundamental in applying inheritance to the construction of reusable, extendible software.*

But inheritance promotes tight coupling. In programming, we like to remove these tight couplings. Robert C. Martin improved the definition and made it polymorphic OCP. His proposal uses abstract base classes with protocols instead of a superclass to allow different implementations. These protocols are closed for modification, and they provide another level of abstraction that enables loose coupling. In this chapter, we'll follow Robert C. Martin's idea that promotes polymorphic OCP.

Note   In the final chapter of this book, I describe some common terms including *cohesion* and *coupling*. If required, you can take a quick look at them.

Initial Program

Assume that there is a small group of students who appear in a certification examination. To demonstrate this, I choose a small number of participants. It helps you to focus on the principle, not unnecessary details. Sam, Bob, John, and Kate are the four students in this example. They all belong to the Student class. To make a Student class instance, you supply a name, registration number, and marks obtained in the examination. You also mention whether a student belongs to the Science stream or the Arts stream. So, you will see the following lines of code in the upcoming example:

```
Student sam = new("Sam", "R001", 81.5, "Science");
Student bob = new("Bob", "R002", 72, "Science");
Student john = new("John", "R003", 71, "Arts");
Student kate = new("Kate", "R004", 66.5, "Arts");
```

Author's Note: In my book *Java Design Patterns* (3rd Edition), I showed individual subjects such as computer science, physics, history, and English under different streams. You can understand that computer science and physics belong to the Science stream and the other two belong to the Arts stream. For simplicity, I have ignored this activity in this chapter. Here, I mention the streams directly and refer to them as departments.

Suppose you start with two instance methods in this example. The DisplayResult() displays the result with all the necessary details of a student, and the EvaluateDistinction() method evaluates whether a student is eligible for a distinction certificate. I assume that if a student from the science department scores above 80 in this examination, they get the certificate with distinction. But the criterion for a student from the arts department is slightly relaxed. Here the student gets the distinction if their score is above 70.

I assume that you do not like to place DisplayResult() and EvaluateDistinction() in the same class (let us call this class Student). Here are some possible reasons behind this decision:

- First, you'll violate the SRP when you place both the DisplayResult() and the EvaluateDistinction() methods inside the same class.

- In the future, the examining authority can change the distinction criteria. In this case, you need to change the EvaluateDistinction() method. Does this solve the problem? In the current situation, the answer is yes. But a college authority can change the distinction criteria again. How many times will you modify the EvaluateDistinction() method?

- Remember that each time you modify the method, you need to write/ modify the existing test cases too.

You can see that every time the distinction criteria changes, you need to modify the EvaluateDistinction() method in the Student class. *So, this class does not follow the SRP, and it is also not closed for modification.*

Once you understand these problems, you start with a better design that follows the SRP. Here are the main characteristics of the design:

- In the following program, Student and DistinctionDecider are two different classes.

- The DistinctionDecider class contains the EvaluateDistinction() method in this example.

- You understand that to show the details of a student, you can override the ToString() method, instead of using a separate method, DisplayResult(). So, inside the Student class, you see the ToString() method now.

- There is a Helper class with a method called MakeStudentList(). Inside the client code, you'll see the following line:

  ```
  List<Student> enrolledStudents =   Helper.MakeStudentList();
  ```

- The MakeStudentList() method creates a list of students. It helps me to avoid repetitive code for each student. You use this list to print the student's details one by one. You also use the same list to invoke EvaluateDistinction() to identify the students who have received the distinction.

Demonstration 3

Here is the complete demonstration.

POINTS TO NOTE

You'll see me using raw-string literals in this program. It is a C# 11 preview feature. I have used this new feature in many programs in this book so that you can be familiar with it. I like it because it is easier to read and it more closely resembles the output text.

```
Console.WriteLine("*** A demo without OCP.***");
List<Student> enrolledStudents =
 Helper.MakeStudentList();

// Display results.
Console.WriteLine("===Results:===");
foreach (Student student in enrolledStudents)
{
    Console.WriteLine(student);
}

// Evaluate distinctions.
DistinctionDecider distinctionDecider = new();
Console.WriteLine("===Distinctions:===");
foreach (Student student in enrolledStudents)
{
    distinctionDecider.EvaluateDistinction(student);
}

class Student
{
    internal string name;
    internal string registrationNumber;
    internal string department;
    internal double score;
    public Student(
     string name,
     string registrationNumber,
     double score,
     string department)
    {
        this.name = name;
        this.registrationNumber = registrationNumber;
        this.score = score;
        this.department = department;
    }
```

```csharp
    // Using C# 11 feature: Raw string literals
    public override string ToString()
    {
        return ($"""
        Name: {name}
        Reg Number: {registrationNumber}
        Dept: {department}
        Score: {score}
        *******
        """);
    }
}
class DistinctionDecider
{
    public void EvaluateDistinction(Student student)
    {

        if (student.department == "Science")
        {
            if (student.score > 80)
            {
                Console.WriteLine($"
                {student.registrationNumber}
                has received a distinction in
                science.");
            }
        }

        if (student.department == "Arts")
        {
            if (student.score > 70)
            {
                Console.WriteLine($"
                {student.registrationNumber}
                has received a distinction in
                arts.");
```

```
        }
      }
    }
}

class Helper
{
  public static List<Student> MakeStudentList()
  {
    Student sam = new("Sam", "R001", 81.5, "Science");
    Student bob = new("Bob", "R002", 72, "Science");
    Student john = new("John", "R003", 71, "Arts");
    Student kate = new("Kate", "R004", 66.5, "Arts");
    List<Student> students = new()
    {
     sam,
     bob,
     john,
     kate
     };
     return students;
  }
}
```

Output

Here is the output:

```
*** A demo without OCP.***
===Results:===
Name: Sam
Reg Number: R001
Dept: Science
Score: 81.5
******
Name: Bob
Reg Number: R002
```

```
Dept: Science
Score: 72
******
Name: John
Reg Number: R003
Dept: Arts
Score: 71
******
Name: Kate
Reg Number: R004
Dept: Arts
Score: 66.5
******
===Distinctions:===
R001 has received a distinction in science.
R003 has received a distinction in arts.
```

Analysis

Now you have followed the SRP. If, in the future, the examining authority changes the distinction criteria, you do not touch the Student class. So, this part is closed for modification. It solves one part of the problem. Now think about another future possibility:

- The college authority can introduce a new stream such as commerce and set a new distinction criterion for this stream.

You need to make some obvious changes again. For example, you need to modify the EvaluateDistinction() method and add another if statement to consider commerce students. Now the question is, is it OK to modify the EvaluateDistinction() method in this manner? Remember that each time you modify the method, you need to test the entire code workflow again.

You understand the problem now. In demonstration 3, every time the distinction criteria changes, you need to modify the EvaluateDistinction() method in the DistinctionDecider class. **So, this class is not closed for modification.**

Better Program

To tackle this problem, you can write a better program. The following program shows such an example. I write this program following the OCP principle that suggests we *write code segments (such as classes or methods) that are open for extension but closed for modification.*

Note   The OCP can be achieved in different ways, but abstraction is the heart of this principle. If you can design your application following the OCP, your application is flexible and extensible. It is not always easy to fully implement this principle, but partial OCP compliance too can generate greater benefit to you. Also notice that I started demonstration 3 following the SRP. If you do not follow the OCP, you may end up with a class that performs multiple tasks, which means the SRP is broken too.

This time we need to tackle the evaluation method for distinction in a better way. So, I create an interface IDistinctionDecider that contains a method EvaluateDistinction. Here is the interface:

```
interface IDistinctionDecider
{
    void EvaluateDistinction(Student student);
}
```

The ArtsDistinctionDecider and ScienceDistinctionDecider implement this interface and override the IDistinctionDecider method to serve their purpose. Here is the code segment for this. The different criteria for each class are shown in bold.

```
class ArtsDistinctionDecider : IDistinctionDecider
{
    public void EvaluateDistinction(Student student)
    {
        if (student.score > 70)
        {
            Console.WriteLine($"
              {student.registrationNumber} has received
```

```
            a distinction in arts.");
        }
    }
}

class ScienceDistinctionDecider : IDistinctionDecider
{
    public void EvaluateDistinction(Student student)
    {
        if (student.score > 80)
        {
            Console.WriteLine($"
            {student.registrationNumber} has received
            a distinction in science.");
        }
    }
}
```

The previous code segment clearly shows the distinction criteria in different streams. So, I remove the department field from the Student class now.

In addition to these changes, this time, I enroll science students and arts students separately. This is why the Helper class contains two methods, MakeScienceStudentList() and MakeArtsStudentList(), respectively. The remaining code is easy, and you should not have any trouble understanding the following demonstration now.

Demonstration 4

Here is the modified program:

```
Console.WriteLine("*** A demo that follows OCP.***");
List<Student> scienceStudents = Helper.MakeScienceStudentList();
List<Student> artsStudents = Helper.MakeArtsStudentList();

Console.WriteLine("===Results:===");
foreach (Student student in scienceStudents)
{
    Console.WriteLine(student);
}
```

```
foreach (Student student in artsStudents)
{
    Console.WriteLine(student);
}

Console.WriteLine("===Distinctions:===");

// For the Science stream students.
IDistinctionDecider distinctionDecider = new
  ScienceDistinctionDecider();
foreach (Student student in scienceStudents)
{
    distinctionDecider.EvaluateDistinction(student);
}

// For the Arts stream students.
distinctionDecider = new ArtsDistinctionDecider();
foreach (Student student in artsStudents)
{
    distinctionDecider.EvaluateDistinction(student);
}
class Student
{
    internal string name;
    internal string registrationNumber;
    internal double score;
    public Student(
      string name,
      string registrationNumber,
      double score)
    {
        this.name = name;
        this.registrationNumber = registrationNumber;
        this.score = score;
```

```csharp
    }
    public override string ToString()
    {
        return ($"""
        Name: {name}
        Reg Number: {registrationNumber}
        Score: {score}
        *******
        """);
    }
}

interface IDistinctionDecider
{
    void EvaluateDistinction(Student student);
}
class ArtsDistinctionDecider : IDistinctionDecider
{
    public void EvaluateDistinction(Student student)
    {
        if (student.score > 70)
        {
            Console.WriteLine($"
              {student.registrationNumber} has received
              a distinction in arts.");
        }
    }
}

class ScienceDistinctionDecider : IDistinctionDecider
{
    public void EvaluateDistinction(Student student)
    {
        if (student.score > 80)
        {
            Console.WriteLine($"
              {student.registrationNumber} has received
```

```
                a distinction in science.");
            }
        }
}

class Helper
{
  public static List<Student> MakeScienceStudentList()
    {
      Student sam = new("Sam", "R001", 81.5);
      Student bob = new("Bob", "R002", 72);
      List<Student> students = new()
      {
        sam,
        bob
      };
      return students;
    }
  public static List<Student> MakeArtsStudentList()
    {
      Student john = new("John", "R003", 71);
      Student kate = new("Kate", "R004", 66.5);
      List<Student> students = new()
      {
        john,
        kate
      };
      return students;
    }
}
```

Output

Notice that the output is the same except the first line that says this program follows the OCP.

```
*** A demo that follows OCP.***
===Results:===
Name: Sam
Reg Number: R001
Score: 81.5
*******
Name: Bob
Reg Number: R002
Score: 72
*******
Name: John
Reg Number: R003
Score: 71
*******
Name: Kate
Reg Number: R004
Score: 66.5
*******
===Distinctions:===
R001 has received a distinction in science.
R003 has received a distinction in arts.
```

Analysis

What are the key advantages now? The following points tell you the answer:

- The Student class and IDistinctionDecider both are unchanged for any future changes in the distinction criteria. They are closed for modification.

- Notice that every participant follows the SRP.

- If you consider students from a different stream such as commerce, you can add a new derived class, say `CommerceDistinctionDecider`, that can implement the `IDistinctionDecider` interface and set new distinction criteria for commerce students.

- Using this approach, you avoid an `if-else` chain (shown in demonstration 3). This chain could grow if you consider new streams such as commerce. In cases like this, avoiding a big `if-else` chain is considered a better practice. This is because by avoiding the `if-else` chains, you lower the cyclomatic complexity of a program and produce better code. (Cyclomatic complexity is a software metric to indicate the complexity of a program. It indicates the number of paths through a particular piece of code. So, in simple terms, by lowering the cyclomatic complexity, you make your code easily readable and testable.)

I'll finish this section with Robert C. Martin's suggestion. In his book *Clean Architecture*, he gave us a simple formula: if you want component A to protect from component B, component B should depend on component A. Now the question is, why do we give component A such importance? It is because we may want to put the most important rules in it.

It is time to study the next principle.

Liskov Substitution Principle

This principle originated from the work of Barbara Liskov in 1988. ***The LSP says that you should be able to substitute a parent (or base) type with a subtype***. This means that in a program segment, you can use a derived class instead of its base class without altering the correctness of the program.

Can you recall how you use inheritance? There is a base class, and you create one (or more) derived classes from it. Then you can add new methods to the derived classes. As long as you directly use the derived class method with a derived class object, everything is fine. A problem may occur, though, if you try to get the polymorphic behavior without following the LSP. How? You'll see a detailed discussion with examples in this chapter.

Let me give you a brief idea. Assume that there are two classes in which B is the base class and D is the subclass (of B). Furthermore, assume that there is a method that accepts a reference of B as an argument, something like the following:

```
public void SomeMethod(B b){
    // Some code
}
```

This method works fine until the point you pass a B instance to it. But what happens if you pass a D instance instead of a B instance? Ideally, the program should not fail. This is because you use the concept of polymorphism and you say that D is basically a B type since class D inherits from class B. A common example is when we say a soccer player is also a player, where we consider the Player class is a parent type/supertype of Soccer Player.

Now see what the LSP suggests to us. It says that SomeMethod should not misbehave/fail if you pass a D instance instead of a B instance to it. But it may happen if you do not write your code following the LSP. The concept will be clearer to you when you go through the upcoming example.

Note   Polymorphic code shows your expertise, but remember that it's the developer's responsibility to implement polymorphic behavior properly and avoid unwanted outcomes.

Initial Program

Let me show you an example that I see every month: I use an online payment portal to pay my electricity bill. Since I am a registered user, when I raise a payment request in this portal, it shows my previous payment(s) too. Let us consider a simplified example based on this real-life scenario.

Assume that you also have a payment portal where a registered user can raise a payment request. You use the method ProcessNewPayment() for this. In this portal, you can also show the user's last payment detail using a method called LoadPreviousPaymentInfo(). Here is a sample code segment for this:

```
interface IPayment
{
    void LoadPreviousPaymentInfo();
    void ProcessNewPayment();
}
class RegisteredUser : IPayment
{
    readonly string name = string.Empty;
    public RegisteredUser(string name)
    {
        this.name = name;
    }
    public void LoadPreviousPaymentInfo()
    {
        Console.WriteLine($"Retrieving {name}'s last
          payment details.");
    }

    public void ProcessNewPayment()
    {
        Console.WriteLine($"Processing {name}'s
          current payment request.");
    }
}
```

Furthermore, let's assume you create a helper class PaymentHelper to display all previous payments and new payment requests of these users. You use ShowPreviousPayments() and ProcessNewPayments() for these activities. These methods call LoadPreviousPaymentInfo() and ProcessNewPayment() on the respective IPayment instances. Here is the PaymentHelper class for your instant reference:

```
class PaymentHelper
{
    readonly List<IPayment> users = new();
    public void AddUser(IPayment user)
    {
```

```
        users.Add(user);
    }
    public void ShowPreviousPayments()
    {
        foreach (IPayment user in users)
        {
            user.LoadPreviousPaymentInfo();
            Console.WriteLine("------");
        }
    }
    public void ProcessNewPayments()
    {
        foreach (IPayment user in users)
        {
            user.ProcessNewPayment();
            Console.WriteLine("**********");
        }
    }
}
```

Inside the client code, you create two users and show their current payment requests along with previous payments. Everything is OK so far.

Demonstration 5

Here is the complete demonstration:

```
Console.WriteLine("***A demo without LSP.***");
PaymentHelper helper = new();

// Instantiating two registered users.
RegisteredUser robin = new("Robin");
RegisteredUser jack = new("Jack");

// Adding the users to the helper.
helper.AddUser(robin);
helper.AddUser(jack);
```

```csharp
// Processing the payments using
// the helper class instance.
helper.ShowPreviousPayments();
helper.ProcessNewPayments();
interface IPayment
{
    void LoadPreviousPaymentInfo();
    void ProcessNewPayment();
}
class RegisteredUser : IPayment
{
    readonly string name = string.Empty;
    public RegisteredUser(string name)
    {
        this.name = name;
    }
    public void LoadPreviousPaymentInfo()
    {
        Console.WriteLine($"Retrieving {name}'s last
          payment details.");
    }

    public void ProcessNewPayment()
    {
        Console.WriteLine($"Processing {name}'s
          current payment request.");
    }
}

class PaymentHelper
{
    readonly List<IPayment> users = new();
    public void AddUser(IPayment user)
    {
        users.Add(user);
    }
```

```
    public void ShowPreviousPayments()
    {
        foreach (IPayment user in users)
        {
            user.LoadPreviousPaymentInfo();
            Console.WriteLine("------");
        }
    }
    public void ProcessNewPayments()
    {
        foreach (IPayment user in users)
        {
            user.ProcessNewPayment();
            Console.WriteLine("**********");
        }
    }
}
```

Output

Here is the output:

```
***A demo without LSP.***
Retrieving Robin's last payment details.
------
Retrieving Jack's last payment details.
------
Processing Robin's current payment request.
**********
Processing Jack's current payment request.
**********
```

This program seems to be fine. ***Now assume that you have a new requirement that says you need to support guest users in the future.*** You understand that you can process a guest user's payment request, but you do not show his last payment detail. So, you create the following class that implements the IPayment interface:

```
class GuestUser : IPayment
{
    readonly string name = string.Empty;
    public GuestUser()
    {
        name = "guest user";
    }

    public void LoadPreviousPaymentInfo()
    {
        throw new NotImplementedException();
    }

    public void ProcessNewPayment()
    {
        Console.WriteLine($"Processing {name}'s
          current payment request.");
    }
}
```

Inside the client code, you create a guest user instance now and try to use your helper class in the same manner. Here is the new client code (notice the changes in bold). For your easy understanding, I have added a comment to draw your attention to the code that causes the problem now.

```
Console.WriteLine("***A demo without LSP.***");
PaymentHelper helper = new();

// Instantiating two registered users
RegisteredUser robin = new("Robin");
RegisteredUser jack = new("Jack");

// Adding the users to usermanager
helper.AddUser(robin);
helper.AddUser(jack);

GuestUser guestUser1 = new();
helper.AddUser(guestUser1);
```

```
// Processing the payments using
// the helper class.
// You can see the problem now.
helper.ShowPreviousPayments();
helper.ProcessNewPayments();
```

This time you get a surprise and encounter an exception. See Figure 4-1.

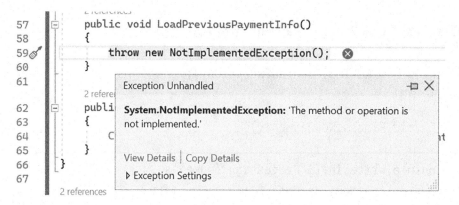

Figure 4-1. *The program encounters the NotImplementedException*

Though GuestUser implements IPayment, it causes PaymentHelper to break. You can understand that the following loop causes this trouble:

```
 foreach (IPayment user in users)
{
  user.LoadPreviousPaymentInfo();
  Console.WriteLine("------");
}
```

In every iteration, you have called the method LoadPreviousPaymentInfo() on the respective IPayment object, and the exception is raised for the GuestUser instance. The previous working solution does not work now because the GuestUser violates the LSP. What is the solution? Go to the next section.

Better Program

The first obvious solution that may come into your mind is to employ an `if-else` chain to verify whether the IPayment instance is a GuestUser or a RegisteredUser. It is a bad solution because if you have another special type of user, you again verify it inside the `if-else` chain. *Most importantly, you violate the OCP each time you modify the existing class using this if-else chain.* So, let us search for a better solution.

Demonstration 6

In this program, I remove the ProcessNewPayment() method from the IPayment interface. I place this method into another interface, INewPayment. As a result, now I have two interfaces with specific operations. Since all types of users can raise a new payment request, the concrete classes RegisteredUser and GuestUser both implement the INewPayment interface. But you show the last payment detail for the registered users only. So, the RegisteredUser class implements the IPayment interface. I always advocate for a proper name. Since IPayment contains the LoadPreviousPaymentInfo() method, it makes sense that you choose a better name, say IPreviousPayment instead of IPayment. I have adjusted these new names in the helper class too. Here is the complete demonstration:

```
Console.WriteLine("***A demo that follows LSP.***");
PaymentHelper helper = new();

// Instantiating two registered users.
RegisteredUser robin = new("Robin");
RegisteredUser jack = new("Jack");

// Adding the info to the helper.
helper.AddPreviousPayment(robin);
helper.AddPreviousPayment(jack);
helper.AddNewPayment(robin);
helper.AddNewPayment(jack);

// Instantiating a guest user.
GuestUser guestUser1 = new();
helper.AddNewPayment(guestUser1);
```

```
// Retrieve all the previous payments
// of registered users.
helper.ShowPreviousPayments();

// Process all new payment requests
// from all users.
helper.ProcessNewPayments();

interface IPreviousPayment
{
    void LoadPreviousPaymentInfo();
}
interface INewPayment
{
    void ProcessNewPayment();
}
class RegisteredUser : IPreviousPayment, INewPayment
{
    readonly string name = String.Empty;
    public RegisteredUser(string name)
    {
        this.name = name;
    }
    public void LoadPreviousPaymentInfo()
    {
        Console.WriteLine($"Retrieving {name}'s last
          payment details.");
    }

    public void ProcessNewPayment()
    {
        Console.WriteLine($"Processing {name}'s
          current payment request.");
    }
}
```

```csharp
class GuestUser : INewPayment
{
    readonly string name = string.Empty;
    public GuestUser()
    {
        this.name = "guest user";
    }

    public void ProcessNewPayment()
    {
        Console.WriteLine($"Processing a {name}'s
          current payment request.");
    }
}

class PaymentHelper
{
  readonly List<IPreviousPayment> previousPayments = new();
  readonly List<INewPayment> newPaymentRequests = new();
  public void AddPreviousPayment(IPreviousPayment previousPayment)
   {
     previousPayments.Add(previousPayment);
   }

  public void AddNewPayment(INewPayment newPaymentRequest)
   {
     newPaymentRequests.Add(newPaymentRequest);
   }
  public void ShowPreviousPayments()
   {
     foreach (IPreviousPayment user in previousPayments)
       {
         user.LoadPreviousPaymentInfo();
         Console.WriteLine("------");
       }
   }
```

```
   public void ProcessNewPayments()
   {
      foreach (INewPayment payment in newPaymentRequests)
      {
         payment.ProcessNewPayment();
         Console.WriteLine("**********");
      }
   }
}
```

Output

Here is the output:

```
***A demo that follows LSP.***
Retrieving Robin's last payment details.
------
Retrieving Jack's last payment details.
------
Processing Robin's current payment request.
**********
Processing Jack's current payment request.
**********
Processing a guest user's current payment request.
**********
```

Analysis

What are the key changes? Notice that in demonstration 5, ShowPreviousPayments() and ProcessNewPayments() both processed IPayment instances. Now ShowPreviousPayments() processes IPreviousPayment instances, and ProcessNewPayments() processes INewPayment instances. This new structure solves the problem that we faced in demonstration 5.

Interface Segregation Principle

You often see a fat interface that contains many methods. A class that implements the interface may not need all these methods. Now the question is, why does the interface contain all these methods? One possible answer is to support some of the implementing classes of this interface. But this should not be the case, and this is the area that the ISP focuses on. It suggests not polluting an interface with these unnecessary methods only to support one (or some) of the implementing classes of this interface. The idea is that *a client should not depend on a method that it does not use*. Once you understand this principle, you'll identify that I have already used ISP when I showed you a better design following the LSP. For now, let us consider an example with a full focus on the ISP.

POINTS TO REMEMBER

Note the following points before you proceed further:

- A client means any class that uses another class (or interface).

- The word *Interface* of the interface segregation principle is not limited to a C# interface. It applies to any base class interface, such as an abstract class or a simple base class.

- Many examples across different programming languages explain the violation of the ISP with an emphasis on throwing an exception such as `NotImplementedException()` in C# or `UnsupportedOperationException()` in Java. In demonstration 7, I also demonstrated to you such an example. It helps me to show you the disadvantages of an approach that does not follow the ISP (and the LSP).

- ISP suggests your class should not depend on interface methods that it does not use. This statement will make more sense to you when you go through the following example.

Initial Program

Assume that you need to write a program that deals with different kinds of printers. Initially, you probably thought of a printer that can print documents as well as send fax. For simplicity, let's call it an AdvancedPrinter. So, you start with an interface IPrinter that has two methods, say PrintDocument() and SendFax(), and then you write the following code segment:

```
interface IPrinter
{
    void PrintDocument();
    void SendFax();
}

class AdvancedPrinter : IPrinter
{
    public void PrintDocument()
    {
        Console.WriteLine("An advanced printer prints the document.");
    }
    public void SendFax()
    {
        Console.WriteLine("An advanced printer sends the fax.");
    }
}
```

Later you discover that there can be more types of printers such as a basic printer that supports only the print activities. So, you create a class BasicPrinter that inherits from the IPrinter interface. Now you need to implement the interface method SendFax(). Since this printer cannot send a fax, you use NotImplementedException() inside the method body. The following code demonstrates this:

```
class BasicPrinter : IPrinter
{
    public void PrintDocument()
    {
```

```
        Console.WriteLine("A basic printer prints the document.");
    }

    public void SendFax()
    {
        throw new NotImplementedException();
    }
}
```

Figure 4-2 shows the simple class diagram for the current situation.

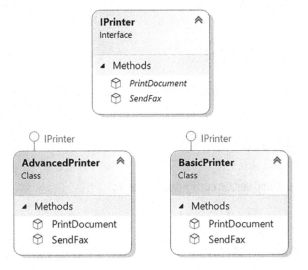

Figure 4-2. *The Printer class hierarchy*

Though everything is OK so far, with this kind of design, you may face trouble in the future. To illustrate this, let me show you a complete program and analyze it further. Do not worry! You'll see a better program shortly.

Demonstration 7

Here is the complete demonstration that does not follow the ISP:

```
Console.WriteLine("***A demo without ISP.***");
IPrinter printer = new AdvancedPrinter();
printer.PrintDocument();
printer.SendFax();
```

```
printer = new BasicPrinter();
printer.PrintDocument();
//printer.SendFax(); // Will throw exception

interface IPrinter
{
    void PrintDocument();
    void SendFax();
}

class BasicPrinter : IPrinter
{
    public void PrintDocument()
    {
        Console.WriteLine("A basic printer prints the document.");
    }

    public void SendFax()
    {
        throw new NotImplementedException();
    }
}
class AdvancedPrinter : IPrinter
{
    public void PrintDocument()
    {
        Console.WriteLine("An advanced printer prints the document.");
    }
    public void SendFax()
    {
        Console.WriteLine("An advanced printer sends the fax.");
    }
}
```

```
An advanced printer prints the document.
An advanced printer sends the fax.
A basic printer prints the document.
```

Analysis

This program suffers from various issues. First and most important, a change to the SendFax() method in the AdvancedPrinter can force the interface Printer to change, which in turn forces the BasicPrinter code to recompile. This situation is always unwanted.

Now you ask me, ***why does a user invite the problem in the first place? Or, why does a user need to change a base class (or, an interface)?*** To answer this, assume that you want to show which type of fax you are using in a later development phase. We know that there are different variations of fax methods, such as LanFax, InternetFax (or, EFax), and AnalogFax. So, earlier, the SendFax() method did not use any parameter, but now it needs to accept a parameter to show the type of fax it uses.

To demonstrate this further, let us suppose you have a fax hierarchy that may look like the following:

```
interface IFax
  {
      void FaxType();
  }
  class LanFax : IFax
  {
      public void FaxType()
      {
          Console.WriteLine("Using lanfax to send the fax.");
      }
  }
  class EFax : IFax
  {
```

```
    public void FaxType()
    {
        Console.WriteLine("Using internet
         fax(efax) to send the fax.");
    }
}
```

To use this inheritance chain, let us assume you update the original SendFax() in AdvancedPrinter. So, you modify the SendFax() method to SendFax (IFax faxType) in the AdvancedPrinter class, which demands you to change the interface IPrinter. When you do this, you need to update BasicPrinter class too to accommodate this change. In short, in this program, if you change the SendFax() method signature in AdvancedPrinter, you need to adjust the change in IPrinter, which causes BasicPrinter to change and recompile. **Now you see the problem!**

It is not the end! Assume that to support another printer that can print, fax, and photocopy, you add a photocopying method in the IPrinter interface. Now both the existing clients, BasicPrinter and AdvancedPrinter, need to accommodate the change. This is why when you see a fat interface, you should ask yourself the following question: are all these methods required for the clients? If not, split the interface into smaller interfaces to ensure no client needs to implement unnecessary methods.

Let us investigate the side effects of this problematic design. Inside the client code, you cannot write polymorphic code like the following (the problematic lines are shown in bold with supportive comments):

```
IPrinter printer = new AdvancedPrinter();
printer.PrintDocument();
printer.SendFax();

printer = new BasicPrinter();
printer.PrintDocument();
//printer.SendFax(); // Will throw exception
```

Or, you cannot write something like this:

```
List<IPrinter> printers = new()
{
 new AdvancedPrinter(),
```

```
 new BasicPrinter()
 };
foreach (IPrinter device in printers)
{
    device.PrintDocument();
    //device.SendFax(); // Will throw exception
}
```

In both these cases, you will see runtime exceptions.

Better Program

Now you have enough reasons to find a better solution. You understand that there are two different activities: one is to print some document, and the other one is to send the fax. So, in the upcoming example, I create two interfaces, IPrinter and IFaxDevice. The IPrinter contains the PrintDocument() method, and the IFaxDevice contains SendFax() method. The idea is simple:

- The class that wants print functionality implements the IPrinter interface, and the class that wants fax functionality implements the IFaxDevice interface.

- If a class wants both these functionalities, it implements both these interfaces.

Note   You should not assume that ISP says an interface should have only one method. In my example, there are two methods in the IPrinter interface, and the BasicPrinter class needs only one of them. That is the reason you see the segregated interfaces with a single method only.

Demonstration 8

Following the ISP, here is a better program for you:

```
Console.WriteLine("***A demo that follows ISP.***");
IPrinter printer = new BasicPrinter();
printer.PrintDocument();
```

```
printer = new AdvancedPrinter();
printer.PrintDocument();

IFaxDevice faxDevice = new AdvancedPrinter();
faxDevice.SendFax();

interface IPrinter
{
    void PrintDocument();
}
interface IFaxDevice
{
    void SendFax();
}
class BasicPrinter : IPrinter
{
    public void PrintDocument()
    {
        Console.WriteLine("A basic printer prints the document.");
    }
}
class AdvancedPrinter : IPrinter, IFaxDevice
{
    public void PrintDocument()
    {
        Console.WriteLine("An advanced printer prints the document.");
    }
    public void SendFax()
    {
        Console.WriteLine("An advanced printer sends the fax.");
    }
}
```

```
***A demo that follows ISP.***
A basic printer prints the document.
An advanced printer prints the document.
An advanced printer sends the fax.
```

Analysis

I often hear the question, what happens if I use a default method inside the interface? If the same question has come to your mind, let me tell you:

- The foremost point is that before C# 8, interfaces couldn't have default methods. All those methods were abstract by default.

- Second, if you use a default method inside the interface or an abstract class, the method is available for use in the derived classes. This kind of practice can violate the OCP and the LSP, which in turn causes hard maintenance and reusability issues. For example, if you provide a default fax method in an interface (or an abstract class), the BasicPrinter must override it by saying something similar to the following:

```
public void SendFax()
{
   throw new NotImplementedException();
}
```

You saw the potential problem with this!

- You can still argue, what happens if I use an empty method, instead of throwing the exception? Yes, the code will work, but for me, providing an empty method for a feature that is not supported at all is not a good solution in a case like this. From my point of view, it is misleading because the client sees no change in output when invoking a valid method.

Note   An alternative technique to implement the ISP is to use the *delegation* technique. The discussion of this is beyond the scope of this book. But you can remember the following point: delegations increase the runtime (it can be small, but it is nonzero for sure) of an application that can affect the performance of the application. Also, in a particular design, a delegated call can create some additional objects too. The unnecessary creation of objects can cause trouble for you because they occupy some memory blocks. So, if you make an application that needs to run using a very small memory (such as a real-time embedded system), you should be careful enough before you create an extra object.

Dependency Inversion Principle

DIP tells two important things:

- A high-level concrete class should not depend on a low-level concrete class. Instead, both should depend on abstractions.

- Abstractions should not depend upon details. Instead, the details should depend upon abstractions.

We'll examine both these points.

The reason for the first point is simple. If the low-level class changes, the high-level class may need to adjust the change; otherwise, the application breaks. What does this mean? It says that you should avoid creating a concrete low-level class inside a high-level class. Instead, you should use abstract classes or interfaces. As a result, you remove the tight coupling between the classes.

The second point is also easy to understand when you analyze the case study that I discussed for the ISP. You saw that if an interface needs to change to support one of its clients, other clients can be impacted due to the change. No client likes to see such an application.

So, in your application, if your high-level modules are independent of low-level modules, you can reuse them easily. This idea also helps you design nice frameworks.

Note   In his book *Agile Principles, Patterns and Practices in C#*, Robert C. Martin explains that a traditional software development model (such as structured analysis and design) tended to create software where high-level modules depend on low-level modules. But in OOP, a well-designed program opposes the idea. It inverts the dependency structure that often results from a traditional procedural method. This is the reason he used the word *inversion* in this principle.

Initial Program

Assume that you have a two-layer application. In this application, a user can save an employee ID in a database. Throughout this book, I use console applications. So, to make things simple, I'll again use a console application instead of a Windows Forms application.

Here you see two classes, UserInterface and OracleDatabase. As per their names, the UserInterface represents a user interface (such as a form where a user can type an employee ID and click the Save button to save the id in a database). Similarly, the OracleDatabase is used to mimic an Oracle database. Again, for simplicity, there is no actual database in this application, and there is no code to validate an employee ID. Here our focus is on the DIP only, so those discussions are not important.

Assume that using the SaveEmployeeId() method of the UserInterface, you can save an employee ID to a database. You'll notice the following code segment inside the UserInterface class:

```
public UserInterface()
{
 this.oracleDatabase = new OracleDatabase();
}
public void SaveEmployeeId(string empId)
{
  // Assume that it is valid data.
  // So, I store it in the database.
  oracleDatabase.SaveEmpIdInDatabase(empId);
}
```

You can see that I instantiate an `OracleDatabase` object inside the `UserInterface` constructor. Later I use this object to invoke the `SaveEmpIdInDatabase()` method, which does the actual saving inside the Oracle database. Figure 4-3 shows the high-level class (`UserInterface`) dependency on the low-level class (`OracleDatabase`).

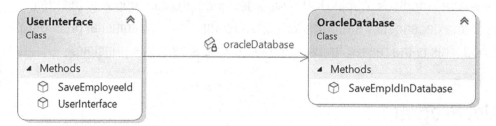

Figure 4-3. *A high-level class, UserInterface, depends on a low-level class, OracleDatabase*

This style of coding is common. But there are some problems. We'll discuss them in the "Analysis" section before I show you a better approach. For now, go through the following program.

Demonstration 9

Here is the complete demonstration that does not follow the DIP:

```
Console.WriteLine("***A demo without DIP.***");
UserInterface userInterface = new();
userInterface.SaveEmployeeId("E001");

class UserInterface
{
    readonly OracleDatabase oracleDatabase;
    public UserInterface()
    {
        this.oracleDatabase = new OracleDatabase();
    }
    public void SaveEmployeeId(string empId)
    {
        // Assuming that this is valid data.
        // So, storing it in the database.
```

```
        oracleDatabase.SaveEmpIdInDatabase(empId);
    }

}
class OracleDatabase
{
    public void SaveEmpIdInDatabase(string empId)
    {
        Console.WriteLine($"The id: {empId} is saved
          in the oracle database.");
    }
}
```

Output

Here is the output:

```
***A demo without DIP.***
The id: E001 is saved in the oracle database.
```

Analysis

The program is simple, but it suffers from the following issues:

- The top-level class (UserInterface) has too much dependency on the bottom-level class (OracleDatabase). These two classes are tightly coupled. So, in the future, if the OracleDatabase class changes, you may need to adjust the changes in the UserInterface. For example, when you change the signature of the SaveEmpIdInDatabase method, you need to adjust the changes in the UserInterface class.

- The low-level class should be available before you write the top-level class. So, you are forced to complete the low-level class before you write or test the high-level class.

- What will you do when you need to support a different database? For example, you may switch from the Oracle database to a MySQL database; or, you may need to support both.

Better Program

In the upcoming program, you'll see the following code segments:

Code segment 1:

```
interface IDatabase
{
  void SaveEmpIdInDatabase(string empId);
}
class OracleDatabase : IDatabase
{
 public void SaveEmpIdInDatabase(string empId)
 {
  Console.WriteLine($"The id: {empId} is saved in the
   Oracle database.");
  }
}
```

Code segment 2:

```
readonly IDatabase database;
public UserInterface(IDatabase database)
{
 this.database = database;
}
```

From these two code segments, you can see that the high-level class `UserInterface` and the low-level class `OracleDatabase` both depend on the abstraction `IDatabase`. This structure fulfills the criteria for the DIP and makes the program efficient.

How? Notice that this time the `UserInterface` class targets the abstraction `IDatabase`, instead of a concrete implementation such as `OracleDatabase`. This gives you the flexibility to consider a new database, such as `MYSQLDatabase`, without altering the existing classes. Figure 4-4 describes the scenario.

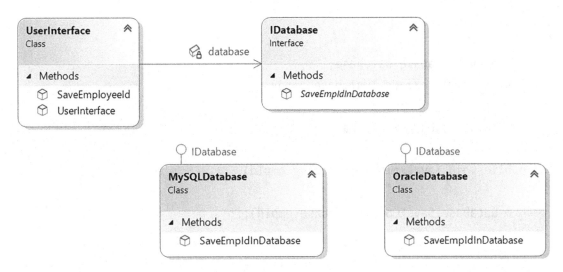

Figure 4-4. *The high-level class UserInterface depends on the abstraction IDatabase*

The second part of the DIP suggests making the IDatabase interface consider the needs of the UserInterface class. This interface does not depend on a low-level class such as OracleDatabase or MySQLDatabase. This is important because if an interface needs to change to support one of its clients, other clients can be impacted due to the change. You saw this when we analyzed the design problems of demonstration 7.

Demonstration 10

To show you the flexibility associated with this design, in addition to OracleDatabase, I have introduced a MYSQLDatabase. Here is the complete program that follows the DIP:

```
Console.WriteLine("***A demo that follows DIP.***");

// Using Oracle now
IDatabase database = new OracleDatabase();
UserInterface userInterface = new(database);
userInterface.SaveEmployeeId("E001");

// Using MySQL now
database = new MySQLDatabase();
userInterface = new UserInterface(database);
userInterface.SaveEmployeeId("E002");
```

```csharp
class UserInterface
{
    readonly IDatabase database;
    public UserInterface(IDatabase database)
    {
        this.database = database;
    }
    public void SaveEmployeeId(string empId)
    {
        database.SaveEmpIdInDatabase(empId);
    }

}
interface IDatabase
{
    void SaveEmpIdInDatabase(string empId);
}
class OracleDatabase : IDatabase
{
    public void SaveEmpIdInDatabase(string empId)
    {
        Console.WriteLine($"The id: {empId} is saved
          in the Oracle database.");
    }
}

class MySQLDatabase : IDatabase
{
    public void SaveEmpIdInDatabase(string empId)
    {
        Console.WriteLine($"The id: {empId} is saved
          in the MySQL database.");
    }
}
```

```
***A demo that follows DIP.***
The id: E001 is saved in the Oracle database.
The id: E002 is saved in the MySQL database.
```

Analysis

You can see that this program resolves all the potential issues of the previous program that I showed you in demonstration 9.

In short, in OOP, I suggest following Robert C. Martin's advice:

> *High-level modules simply should not depend on low-level modules in any way.*

So, when you have a base class and a derived class, your base class should not know about any of its derived classes. But there are a few exceptions to this suggestion. For example, consider the case when your base class needs to restrict the count of the derived class instances at a certain point.

One last point: you can see that in demonstration 10, the UserInterface class constructor accepts a IDatabase parameter. You can provide an additional facility to a user when you use both the constructor and the property inside this class. Here is the sample code for you. To follow the naming convention, I needed to choose the name Database instead of database this time. I also keep the commented code so that you can compare it with the existing code.

```
class UserInterface
{
 //readonly IDatabase database;
 public IDatabase Database { get; set; }
 public UserInterface(IDatabase database)
 {
  //this.database = database;
  this.Database = database;
 }
```

```
public void SaveEmployeeId(string empId)
{
 //database.SaveEmpIdInDatabase(empId);
 Database.SaveEmpIdInDatabase(empId);
}
}
```

What is the benefit? Now you can instantiate a database while instantiating the UserInterface class and change it later using the Database property. Here is the sample code for you, which you can append at the end of the client code to test it:

```
// Additional code for demonstration purpose
userInterface.Database = new OracleDatabase();
userInterface.SaveEmployeeId("E003");
```

You can follow the same technique for similar examples that are used in this book.

Summary

The SOLID principles are the fundamental guidelines in object-oriented design. They are high-level concepts that help you make better software. These are neither rules nor laws, but they help you think of possible scenarios/outcomes in advance. In this chapter, I showed you applications that follow (and do not follow) these principles and discussed the pros and cons.

The SRP says that *a class should have only one reason to change*. Using the SRP, you can write cleaner and less fragile code. You identify the responsibilities and make classes based on each responsibility. What is a responsibility? It is a reason for a change. But you should not assume that a class should have a single method only. If multiple methods help you to achieve a single responsibility, your class can contain all these methods. You are OK to bend this rule based on the nature of possible changes. The reason for this is that if you have too many classes in an application, it is difficult to maintain. But the idea is that when you know this principle and think carefully before you implement a design, you can avoid some typical mistakes that I discussed earlier.

Robert C. Martin mentioned the OCP as the most important object-oriented design principle. The OCP suggests that *software entities (a class, module, method, etc.) should be open for extension but closed for modification*. The idea is if you do not touch a running code, you do not break it. For new features, you add new codes but do not disturb the existing code. This helps you to save time to retest the entire workflow again. Instead, you focus on the newly added code and test that part. This principle is often hard to achieve, but partial OCP compliance too can provide a bigger benefit to you in the long term. In many cases, when you violate OCP, you break the SRP too.

The idea of the LSP is that **you should be able to substitute a parent (or base) type with a subtype.** It is your responsibility to write true polymorphic code using the LSP. Using this principle, you can avoid the long tail of if-else chains and make your code OCP compliant too.

The idea behind ISP is that **a client should not depend on a method that it does not use.** This is why you may need to split a fat interface into multiple interfaces to make a better solution. I have shown you a simple technique to implement the idea. When you do not modify an existing interface (or an abstract class or a simple base class), you follow OCP too. In fact, an ISP compliance application can help you make OCP and LSP compliance applications. You can make an ISP compliance application using the delegation technique, which I did not discuss in this book. But the important point is that when you use the delegation, you increase the runtime (you may say it is negligible, but it is nonzero for sure), which can affect a time-sensitive application. Using delegation, you may create a new object when a client uses the application. It may cause memory issues in certain scenarios.

The DIP suggests two important points for us. **First, a high-level concrete class should not depend on a low-level concrete class. Instead, both should depend on abstractions. Second, the abstractions should not depend upon details. Instead, the details should depend upon abstractions.** When you consider the first part of the suggestion, your application is efficient and flexible; you can consider new concrete implementations in your application. When you analyze the second part of this principle, you understand that you should not change an existing base class or interface to support one of its clients. This can cause another client to break, and you violate OCP in such a case. I analyzed the importance of both these points.

CHAPTER 5

Use the DRY Principle

This chapter discusses the *don't repeat yourself* (DRY) principle. It is another important principle that a professional coder follows when writing a piece of code in an application. The SRP and OCP principles that you learned about in Chapter 4 are also related to the DRY principle. Andy Hunt and Dave Thomas first wrote about this principle in their book *The Pragmatic Programmer*. The DRY principle is stated as follows:

> *Every piece of knowledge must have a single, unambiguous, authoritative representation within a system.*

This may seem complicated when you read it for the first time. The goal of this chapter is to help you understand this principle with a case study.

Reasons for DRY

Code duplication can cause an application to fail. Programmers often call any duplication an *evil* in software. So the question is, why do we see any duplicated code at all? There are a variety of reasons. Here are some examples:

- A programmer cannot resist doing a simple copy/paste, which appears as the shortest path to success.

- The project deadline is approaching. The developer assumes that a certain number of duplicates are OK at this moment. The developer plans to remove these duplicates in the next release but forgets to do so.

- Duplicates are seen in code comments too. Say a developer knows the code very well and does not need the documentation to understand the logic of the code. A new requirement forced the developer to update a portion of the code. So, the developer starts

© Vaskaran Sarcar 2023
V. Sarcar, *Simple and Efficient Programming with C#*, https://doi.org/10.1007/978-1-4842-8737-8_5

working with an existing code and its associated comments. Once the update is done, due to various reasons, the developer forgets to update the associated comments.

- A tester may need to pass the same input to verify various methods in a test suite.

- Sometimes duplicates are hard to avoid. Project standards may require a developer to put duplicate information in the code.

- Suppose your software targets multiple platforms that use different programming languages and/or development environments. In this case, you may need to duplicate shared information (such as methods).

- In addition, a programming language can have a structure that duplicates some information.

In computer science, developers follow many principles to avoid code duplications. For example, database normalization techniques try to eliminate duplicate data. In Chapter 2, you saw that you can put a common method in an abstract base class to avoid duplicating the method in the derived classes.

I must say that finding duplicate code is not always easy. For example, consider the following code segment with two methods.

Code segment 1:

```
public void DisplayCost()
{
 Console.WriteLine("Game name: SuperGame");
 Console.WriteLine("Version:1.0");
 Console.WriteLine("Actual cost is: $1000");
}

public void DisplayCostAfterDiscount()
{
 Console.WriteLine("Game name: SuperGame");
 Console.WriteLine("Version:1.0");
 Console.WriteLine("The discounted price for festive
   season is:$800");
}
```

You can easily see that the initial two lines are common to both of these methods. But the same kind of detection is not straightforward if the duplications are intermixed with other code/comments. For example, consider code segment 2.

Code segment 2:

```
public void DisplayCost()
{
 Console.WriteLine("\AbcCompany SuperGame's price details:");
 Console.WriteLine("Version:1.0 cost is: $1000");
}

public void DisplayCostAfterDiscount()
{
 Console.WriteLine("\AbcCompany offers festive season discount.");
 Console.WriteLine("Discounted price detail:");
 Console.WriteLine("Game: SuperGame. Version: 1.0.
  Discounted price:$800");
}
```

On careful observation, you can find that in both code segments, the company name, game name, and version detail of the software are repeated. In the first code segment, it is easy to find the duplicate code, but in the second code segment, you need to read the code carefully.

These code segments contain only two methods. In a real-world application, you would see a lot of methods, and not all the methods are present in the same file. So, if you spread duplicate information across the files, a simple update can cause the software to show inconsistent behavior.

During an update operation, if you have n number of duplicates, you need n-fold modification, and you cannot miss any of them. This is why you need to be careful about them. Violating the DRY principle causes a WET solution, which commonly stands for "write every time," "write everything twice," "we enjoy typing," or "waste everyone's time." Like the previous chapters, I start with a program that seems fine at the beginning. I then analyze this program and make it better by eliminating redundant code. You can follow the same approach when you encounter a similar situation.

Initial Program

Here is a simplistic example for you. The following are the key assumptions in this program:

- There is game software called SuperGame. You create a class to represent this game.

- The AboutGame() method provides some useful information about this software. For example, it says that the minimum age for using this software is 10. It also shows the current version of the game.

- The DisplayCost() methods specifies the price of the latest version of this software.

- A buyer can get up to a 20 percent discount. The DisplayCostAfterDiscount() method shows the discounted price of the latest software.

Demonstration 1

Assume that someone has written the following program. It compiles and runs successfully. Let's see the output and then read the "Analysis" section.

```
Console.WriteLine("***A demo without the DRY principle. ***");
SuperGame superGame = new ();
superGame.AboutGame();
superGame.DisplayCost();
superGame.DisplayCostAfterDiscount();

class SuperGame
{
    public void AboutGame()
    {
        Console.WriteLine("Game name: SuperGame");
        Console.WriteLine("Minimum age: 10 years and above.");
        Console.WriteLine("Current version: 1.0.");
        Console.WriteLine("It is the AbcCompany product.");
    }
```

```
    public void DisplayCost()
    {
        Console.WriteLine("\nAbcCompany SuperGame's price details:");
        Console.WriteLine("Version:1.0 \nCost:$1000");
    }

    public void DisplayCostAfterDiscount()
    {
        Console.WriteLine("\nAbcCompany offers a festive season discount.");
        Console.WriteLine("Discounted price details:");
        Console.WriteLine("Game: SuperGame. \nVersion:
            1.0 \nDiscounted price: $800");
    }
}
```

Output

Here is the output:

```
***A demo without the DRY principle. ***
Game name: SuperGame
Minimum age: 10 years and above.
Current version: 1.0.
It is the AbcCompany product.

AbcCompany SuperGame's price details:
Version:1.0
Cost: $1000

AbcCompany offers a festive season discount.
Discounted price details:
Game: SuperGame.
Version: 1.0
Discounted price: $800
```

Analysis

Can you see the problems with this program? How many times are you seeing the company name AbcCompany and the version detail in this program? I know that it's a simple program, but consider the more complex case I mentioned earlier. These methods can reside in different modules, and if you needed to update the company information or the version details, you would need to figure out all of those places before you provide the update. This is why the DRY principle needs to be applied.

This program suffers from the use of hard-coded strings. The solution to this problem is straightforward. You can use a single place to contain these strings that appear in multiple parts of your program. Then you share this code segment with other parts of the program. As a result, when you update a string in the shared location, the change reflects properly in every place.

The basic idea is that if you see common code in multiple locations, you separate the common parts from the remaining parts, put them in a single location, and call this common code from other parts of the program. In this way, you avoid the copy/paste technique, which may seem appealing at the beginning but creates problems as time goes on.

Note   There is another principle called the *once and only once* (OAOO) principle, which is similar to the DRY principle. The page at `https://wiki.c2.com/?OnceAndOnlyOnce` states that every declaration of behavior should appear once and only once. So, the OAOO principle is helpful in the context of functional behavior, and you can apply this while refactoring your code. You can think of it as a subset of DRY because the DRY principle is not limited to code and design; you can apply it to other project artifacts as well. For example, you can automate the code integration process instead of repeating it. In simple words, the core ideas of DRY and OAOO are the same.

Can you make demonstration 1 better? Let's look at the following program.

Better Program

This program uses a constructor to initialize the values. You can use these values in the instance methods of the class.

POINTS TO NOTE

You'll see that I have used the raw string literals in the upcoming program. You know that this is a C# 11 preview feature. So, instead of using the following line:

```
Console.WriteLine($"Version:{version} " +
                $"Cost: {actualCost}");
```

I could have used the following to produce the same output:

```
Console.WriteLine($"""
                Version:{version}
                Cost: {actualCost}
                """);
```

Demonstration 2

Here is an improved version:

```
Console.WriteLine("***Demonstration 2: An improved version***");
SuperGame superGame = new ();
superGame.AboutGame();
superGame.DisplayCost();
superGame.DisplayCostAfterDiscount();

class SuperGame
{
    readonly string companyName;
    readonly string gameName;
    readonly double minimumAge;
    readonly string version;
    readonly double actualCost;
    readonly double discountedCost;
    public SuperGame()
    {
        companyName = "AbcCompany";
        gameName = "SuperGame";
        version = "1.0";
```

```
        minimumAge = 10;
        actualCost = 1000;
        discountedCost = 800;
    }

    public void AboutGame()
    {
        Console.WriteLine($"Game name: {gameName}");
        Console.WriteLine($"Minimum age: {minimumAge}
          years and above.");
        Console.WriteLine($"Current version:
          {version}.");
        Console.WriteLine($"It is a {companyName}
          product.");
    }

    public void DisplayCost()
    {
        Console.WriteLine($"\n{companyName}
          SuperGame's price details:");
        Console.WriteLine($"""
                          Version:{version}
                          Cost: {actualCost}
                          """);
    }
    public void DisplayCostAfterDiscount()
    {
        Console.WriteLine($"\n{companyName} offers a
          festive season discount.");
        Console.WriteLine("Discounted price detail:");
        Console.WriteLine($"""
            Game: {gameName}.
            Version: {version}.
            Discounted price: {discountedCost}
            """);
    }
}
```

Output

Here is the output of this program:

```
***Demonstration 2: An improved version***
Game name: SuperGame
Minimum age: 10 years and above.
Current version: 1.0.
It is the AbcCompany product.

AbcCompany SuperGame's price details:
Version:1.0
Cost: 1000

AbcCompany offers a festive season discount.
Discounted price detail:
Game: SuperGame.
Version: 1.0.
Discounted price:800
```

You can see that this program produces the same output except for the first line, which prints that it is an improved version.

Analysis

You can see that the issues with the hard-coded strings are taken care of in demonstration 2. Still, there is some repetition in this example. Notice that the company name is shown in AboutGame(), DisplayCost(), and DisplayCostAfterDiscount(). This was OK for me because I wanted to display the company name in any of the methods that a client may use.

But you can improve this program. The initial version of the software and the company name may not change for a different game (which is made by the same company), but the name of the game and price details are likely to change. So, let's improve the program logic and work further in these areas. In addition, if you understand the SOLID principles from Chapter 4, you know that this program does not follow the SRP.

In short, you may need to update this program in the future due to various reasons. Some of them are as follows:

- The cost of the software can be changed.

- The discounted price can be changed.

- The version detail can be changed.

- The name of the game can be changed.

- Also, consider the case when the company name itself can be changed.

So, I move the `company name`, `game name`, `version`, and `age requirement` into a new class called `GameInfo`. The actual price and the discounted price are moved into a different class called `GamePrice`. In addition, this time I use properties so that you can apply some changes to the initial values at a later stage.

In this upcoming program, when you instantiate a `GameInfo` instance, you supply the name of the game, but before that, you initialize a `GameInfo` instance and a `GamePrice` instance. This activity helps you to instantiate a game instance with the default information stored in `GameInfo` and `GamePrice`. As I said before, you can change these values using various properties of these classes.

Further Improvement

Now let's go through the proposed improvement. You can follow a similar structure to adapt to a new requirement with a small change.

Demonstration 3

Here is an improved version of demonstration 2 (I have kept some comments in to help you understand the concepts):

```
Console.WriteLine("*** Another improved version
  following the DRY principle. ***");

// Initial setup
GameInfo gameInfo = new("SuperGame");
GamePrice gamePrice = new();
```

```
// Create the game instance with the default setup
Game game = new(gameInfo, gamePrice);

// Display the default game detail.
game.AboutGame();
game.DisplayCost();
game.DisplayCostAfterDiscount();
Console.WriteLine("------------");

Console.WriteLine("Changing the game version and price now.");

// Changing some of the game info
gameInfo.Version = "2.0";
gameInfo.MinimumAge = 9.5;

// Changing the game cost
gamePrice.Cost = 1500;
gamePrice.DiscountedCost = 1200;

// Updating the game instance
game = new Game(gameInfo, gamePrice);

// Display the latest detail
game.AboutGame();
game.DisplayCost();
game.DisplayCostAfterDiscount();

class GameInfo
{
    public string CompanyName { get; set; }
    public string GameName { get; set; }
    public string Version { get; set; }
    public double MinimumAge { get; set; }
    public GameInfo(string gameName)
    {
        CompanyName = "AbcCompany";
        GameName = gameName;
        Version = "1.0";
```

```
        MinimumAge = 10.5;
    }
}

class GamePrice
{
    public double Cost { get; set; }
    public double DiscountedCost { get; set; }

    public GamePrice()
    {
        Cost = 1000;
        DiscountedCost = 800;
    }
}

class Game
{
    readonly string companyName;
    readonly string gameName;
    readonly double minimumAge;
    readonly string version;
    readonly double actualCost;
    readonly double discountedCost;
    public Game(GameInfo gameInfo,
                GamePrice gamePrice)
    {
        companyName = gameInfo.CompanyName;
        gameName = gameInfo.GameName;
        version = gameInfo.Version;
        minimumAge = gameInfo.MinimumAge;
        actualCost = gamePrice.Cost;
        discountedCost = gamePrice.DiscountedCost;
    }
    public void AboutGame()
    {
        Console.WriteLine($"Game name: {gameName}");
```

```
    Console.WriteLine($"Minimum age: {minimumAge}
      years and above.");
    Console.WriteLine($"Current version:
     {version}.");
    Console.WriteLine($"It is the {companyName}
      product.");
}
public void DisplayCost()
{
    Console.WriteLine($"\n{companyName}
     {gameName}'s price details:");
    Console.WriteLine($"""
                     Version: {version}
                     Cost: {actualCost}
                     """);
}
public void DisplayCostAfterDiscount()
{
    Console.WriteLine($"\n{companyName} offers a
     festive season discount.");
    Console.WriteLine("Discounted price detail:");
    Console.WriteLine($"""
          Game: {gameName}.
          Version: {version}.
          Discounted price: {discountedCost}
          """);
}
}
```

Output

Here is the new output that reflects the changes in various fields:

```
*** Another improved version following the DRY principle. ***
Game name: SuperGame
Minimum age: 10.5 years and above.
```

```
Current version: 1.0.
It is the AbcCompany product.

AbcCompany SuperGame's price details:
Version:1.0
Cost: 1000

AbcCompany offers a festive season discount.
Discounted price detail:
Game: SuperGame.
Version: 1.0.
Discounted price:800
------------
Changing the game version and price now.
Game name: SuperGame
Minimum age: 9.5 years and above.
Current version: 2.0.
It is the AbcCompany product.

AbcCompany SuperGame's price details:
Version:2.0
Cost: 1500

AbcCompany offers a festive season discount.
Discounted price detail:
Game: SuperGame.
Version: 2.0.
Discounted price:1200
```

Is it the end of the improvements? You know the answer to that. There is no end to improvement; you can always improve your code. You know that a company does not finish with making a single game. A company can create multiple games, but they can share a common format to display information about the games. So, if tomorrow the company wants you to make a new game, say NewPokemonKid, how should you proceed? Will you copy/paste the existing code and start editing? You know that this process is not recommended at all.

You can make this program better if you move the Game, GameInfo, and GamePrice classes to a shared library and use them accordingly. When you do this, you again follow the DRY principle because you do not copy/paste the existing code to make a new game or to enhance a requirement. Instead, you reuse an existing solution that works fine, and using this you indirectly save your test time.

So, I create a class library project called BasicGameInfo and create a namespace, and then I move these classes into a common file, CommonLibrary.cs (I renamed it from class1.cs). I make these classes public so that I can access them from a different file. Creating a namespace was optional for me, but I followed Visual Studio's suggestion here. To make the code more professional, this time I add a few descriptions of these classes too. You can see them in the upcoming demonstration.

For your immediate reference, see the Solution Explorer view in Figure 5-1 where I use a BasicGameInfo project reference in the Demo4_DRYUsingDll project.

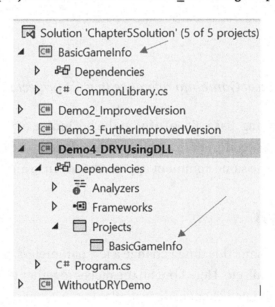

Figure 5-1. *Demo4_DryDemoUsingDll is using the BasicGameInfo project reference*

After I created the project Demo4_DRYUsingDll, I added the BasicGameInfo reference. Figure 5-2 shows you a sample snapshot when I right-click the project dependencies, add the reference, and about to click the OK button.

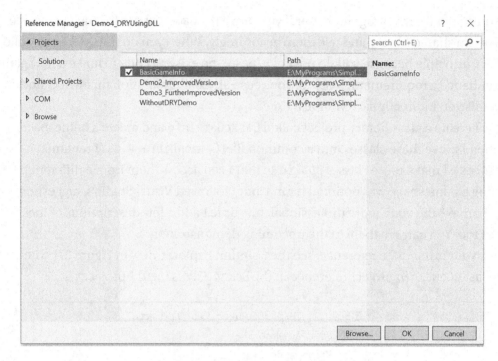

Figure 5-2. *Adding BasicGameInfo reference to a C# project file*

Now you can add using BasicGameInfo; at the beginning of your new file.
This helps you to type less code. For example, you can directly use Game instead of
BasicGameInfo.Game. The same comment applies to GameInfo and GamePrice.

Demonstration 4

To show you a sample demo, this time I change a few parameters, like the name of the
game, version, price detail, etc. Here I put all the pieces together for your easy reference.
You'll notice that this updated client code is similar to the client code that you saw in the
previous demonstration. Here is the complete program:

```
// The content of CommonLibrary.cs

namespace BasicGameInfo
{
    /// <summary>
    /// Provides the company name, game name,
    /// version and the age criteria.
```

```
/// </summary>
public class GameInfo
{
    public string CompanyName { get; set; }
    public string GameName { get; set; }
    public string Version { get; set; }
    public double MinimumAge { get; set; }
    public GameInfo(string gameName)
    {
        CompanyName = "AbcCompany";
        GameName = gameName;
        Version = "1.0";
        MinimumAge = 10.5;
    }
}
/// <summary>
/// Shows the actual price and the
/// discounted price of the game.
/// </summary>
public class GamePrice
{
    public double Cost { get; set; }
    public double DiscountedCost { get; set; }

    public GamePrice()
    {
        Cost = 1000;
        DiscountedCost = 800;
    }
}

/// <summary>
/// Provides different methods to retrieve
/// the game information.
/// </summary>
```

```
public class Game
{
    readonly string companyName;
    readonly string gameName;
    readonly double minimumAge;
    readonly string version;
    readonly double actualCost;
    readonly double discountedCost;
    public Game(GameInfo gameInfo,
      GamePrice gamePrice)
    {
        companyName = gameInfo.CompanyName;
        gameName = gameInfo.GameName;
        version = gameInfo.Version;
        minimumAge = gameInfo.MinimumAge;
        actualCost = gamePrice.Cost;
        discountedCost = gamePrice.DiscountedCost;
    }
    public void AboutGame()
    {
        Console.WriteLine($"Game name:
          {gameName}");
        Console.WriteLine($"Minimum age:
          {minimumAge} years and above.");
        Console.WriteLine($"Current version:
          {version}.");
        Console.WriteLine($"It is a {companyName}
         product.");
    }
    public void DisplayCost()
    {
        Console.WriteLine($"\n{companyName}
          {gameName}'s price details:");
        Console.WriteLine($"""
          Version:{version}
```

```
                Cost: {actualCost}
                """);
        }
        public void DisplayCostAfterDiscount()
        {
            Console.WriteLine($"\n{companyName} offers
                a festive season discount.");
            Console.WriteLine("Discounted price
                detail:");
            Console.WriteLine($"""
                Game: {gameName}.
                Version: {version}.
                Discounted price:{discountedCost}
                """);
        }
    }
}
```

// The content of the new client code

```
using BasicGameInfo;
Console.WriteLine("*** Applying the DRY principle
  using a DLL. ***");

// Initial setup
GameInfo gameInfo = new ("NewPokemonKid");
GamePrice gamePrice = new ();

// Create the game instance with a
// default setup
Game game = new(gameInfo, gamePrice);

// Display the default game detail.
game.AboutGame();
game.DisplayCost();
game.DisplayCostAfterDiscount();

Console.WriteLine("------------");
```

```
Console.WriteLine("Changing the game version and price
  now.");

// Changing some of the game info
gameInfo.Version = "2.1";
gameInfo.MinimumAge = 12.5;

// Changing the game cost
gamePrice.Cost = 3500;
gamePrice.DiscountedCost = 2000;

// Updating the game instance
game = new Game(gameInfo, gamePrice);

// Display the latest detail
game.AboutGame();
game.DisplayCost();
game.DisplayCostAfterDiscount();
```

Output

When you run this program, you get the following output:

```
*** Applying the DRY principle using a DLL. ***
Game name: NewPokemonKid
Minimum age: 10.5 years and above.
Current version: 1.0.
It is a AbcCompany product.

AbcCompany NewPokemonKid's price details:
Version:1.0
Cost: 1000

AbcCompany offers a festive season discount.
Discounted price detail:
Game: NewPokemonKid.
Version: 1.0.
Discounted price:800
------------
```

```
Changing the game version and price now.
Game name: NewPokemonKid
Minimum age: 12.5 years and above.
Current version: 2.1.
It is the AbcCompany product.

AbcCompany NewPokemonKid's price details:
Version:2.1
Cost: 3500

AbcCompany offers a festive season discount.
Discounted price detail:
Game: NewPokemonKid.
Version: 2.1.
Discounted price:2000
```

Once again we get the desired result by following the DRY principle and reusing existing code.

I know what you are thinking. You see a tight coupling between Game and GameInfo/ GamePrice. Yes, that is true. How can you remove this coupling? Since you learned about the DIP in the previous chapter, this should not be a problem for you. I will leave this as an exercise for you.

Summary

Code duplication can cause serious problems for software. Expert programmers often treat these duplications as evils in the software. Why do we see duplicate code? There are a variety of reasons; some of them are attractive, and some of them are hard to avoid. But by removing the redundant code, you make better software that is easier to maintain.

This chapter showed you how to apply the DRY principle. You saw an initial version of a program that was improved multiple times to make it better. Finally, you moved the common code to a shared library.

This principle applies not only to the actual code but also to code comments and test cases. For example, you can make a common input file to test various methods instead of passing the same input repeatedly in every method. When you consider using code comments, try to keep the low-level knowledge in the code and use the comments for high-level explanations. Otherwise, for each update, you need to change both the code and the comments.

You'll probably agree with me that repeated code causes higher development costs and more maintenance problems. The DRY principle discourages those activities. Since it promotes reusability, it accelerates the overall development process in the long run. In short, this principle helps you write cleaner and better code. So, by using this principle, you make better software.

PART III

Make Efficient Applications

Part III consists of four chapters, in which we will develop some useful applications that follow several important design patterns. This part will cover the following:

- How can we use factories to separate a code segment that is more likely to vary from a code segment that is less likely to vary?

- How can we add new features to an application using wrappers?

- How can we use a template method and a hook method together to make an efficient application?

- How can we simplify a complex system using facades?

The software industry is full of patterns and design guidelines. As you continue coding and creating different applications, you will discover their importance and understand when to choose one technique over another. In the preface of the book, I told you about the Pareto principle, or 80-20 rule, which states that 80 percent of outcomes come from 20 percent of all causes. This is why, in this part, I show you the techniques that are commonly used to build real-world applications. Once you master these techniques, you will get a hint about the answer to the following question: what does a professional programmer think before writing a piece of code?

CHAPTER 6

Separate Changeable Code Using Factories

A developer's end goal is to make an application that meets the requirements of the customer. But the code must be easily extensible, maintainable, and stable enough to meet future needs too. It is tough to write the best version of a program on the very first attempt. You may need to analyze the code and refactor it several times. In this chapter, you will see such a scenario and learn how to use factories. To simplify the discussion, I start with a small program. We'll keep analyzing the program and modifying it accordingly.

To make a stable application, an expert programmer attempts to make a loosely coupled system. The programmer tries to identify the code that can vary a bit. Once this is done, the programmer separates that part of the code from the remaining part of the codebase. Factories are best in this type of scenario.

POINTS TO REMEMBER

The obvious question is, what is a factory? In simple words, a *factory* is a code segment that handles the details of an object creation process. Any method that uses a factory is called a *client* of the factory. You should note that a factory can have many clients. These clients can use the factory to get an object, and later as per their needs, they invoke the methods of the object. So, it is up to a client how to use the object that is received from a factory. This is why separating the object creation process into a shared place is beneficial. Otherwise, you end up with duplicate code in multiple clients.

© Vaskaran Sarcar 2023
V. Sarcar, *Simple and Efficient Programming with C#*, https://doi.org/10.1007/978-1-4842-8737-8_6

The Problem Statement

Assume that you write a program to demonstrate the behavior of two different animals, say tigers and cats. But you have a constraint that says *you should not instantiate the animal object inside the client code.* Why do you have this constraint? Here are some reasons:

- You want to hide the instantiation logic from a client. You know that "change" is the only constant in the programming world. Let's see what happens if the object's instantiation logic resides on the client side. When you enhance your application to support a new type of object, you need to update the client code too. This demands retesting the client code as well.

- There may be separate classes with methods that can also create cats or tigers. So, it is better to separate the code that instantiates a cat or a tiger in a shared place. In such a case, it does not matter how many clients use this code. Every client can refer to the common location to instantiate an object.

So, how can you separate the instantiation logic from the client code? You'll see this in the upcoming demonstrations.

Initial Program

Following this requirement, let's suppose that you write the following program that is shown in demonstration 1. Before you go through the complete program, here are some important points:

- In this program, the `AnimalFactory` class is responsible for instantiating an object. It contains a method, called `CreateAnimal()`, to create a tiger or a cat instance.

- The `CreateAnimal()` method is nonstatic. However, you can make it static. I discuss the pros and cons of using a static method in Chapter 14 of this book.

- The AnimalFactory class acts like a factory class in this example. It contains a method, called CreateAnimal(), to create instances. So, you can say that this is the factory method in this example.

- Inside the client code, you instantiate this factory class to get an animal. This is why the client uses the following code to get an animal and display its behavior:

```
AnimalFactory animalFactory = new ();
IAnimal animal = animalFactory.CreateAnimal("cat");
animal.DisplayBehavior();
```

Demonstration 1

Here is the complete program:

```
Console.WriteLine("***Creating animals and learning
  about them. ***");
AnimalFactory animalFactory = new();

IAnimal animal = animalFactory.CreateAnimal("cat");
animal.DisplayBehavior();

animal = animalFactory.CreateAnimal("tiger");
animal.DisplayBehavior();

interface IAnimal
{
    void DisplayBehavior();
}

class Tiger : IAnimal
{
    public Tiger()
    {
        Console.WriteLine("\nA tiger is created.");
    }
    public void DisplayBehavior()
    {
```

```csharp
        Console.WriteLine("""
         It roars.
         It loves to roam in the jungle.
         """);
    }
}

class Cat : IAnimal
{
    public Cat()
    {
        Console.WriteLine("\nA cat is created.");
    }
    public void DisplayBehavior()
    {
        Console.WriteLine("""
         It meows.
         It loves to stay at a home.
         """);
    }
}

class AnimalFactory
{
    public IAnimal CreateAnimal(string animalType)
    {
        IAnimal animal;
        if (animalType.Equals("cat"))
        {
            animal = new Cat();
        }
        else if (animalType.Equals("tiger"))
        {
            animal = new Tiger();
        }
        else
        {
```

```
            Console.WriteLine("You can create either a
               cat or a tiger. ");
            throw new ApplicationException("An unknown
               animal cannot be instantiated.");
        }
        return animal;
    }
}
```

Output

Here is the output:

```
***Creating animals and learning about them. ***

A cat is created.
It meows.
It loves to stay at a home.

A tiger is created.
It roars.
It loves to roam in the jungle.
```

Analysis

The approach you use in demonstration 1 is quite common in programming. In the programming world, this has a name; we call it a ***simple factory pattern***. Now let us analyze this program. Here are the important points:

- You may need to enhance this application, because this application may need to create a different type of animal, say, a monkey, in the future. How can you proceed? You need to modify the AnimalFactory class and increase the if-else chain to consider the monkeys. But when you do this, you violate the OCP, and as a result, you need to retest the AnimalFactory class.

POINTS TO REMEMBER

When you see the `switch` statements, or an `if-else` chain to create different types
of objects in a similar example, you get a clue that you may need to reopen the code to
accommodate future changes. In the worst case, this code is replicated in several parts of an
application. As a result, you keep violating the OCP, which can cause a serious maintenance
problem in the future.

- In this program, Visual Studio shows you a message that says,
  "CA1822: Member 'CreateAnimal' does not access instance data
  and can be marked as static. It also keeps saying: Members that do
  not access instance data or call instance methods can be marked
  as static. After you mark the methods as static, the compiler will
  emit non-virtual call sites to these members. This can give you a
  measurable performance gain for performance-sensitive code."

- I do not consider taking this suggestion now. The reasons are
  simple. First, performance sensitivity is not the key goal right now.
  Second, though a static method allows me to call the method without
  instantiating an object, it has disadvantages too. For example, you
  cannot change the behavior of a static method at runtime. As I said
  earlier, you'll learn about this more in Chapter 14.

Better Program

By following the OCP principle, you can make the program better. So, in the upcoming
demonstration, you will see a new hierarchy. I have kept the comments in to help you
understand the code.

```
#region Factory hierarchy

/// <summary>
/// This class contains the "factory method"
/// </summary>
abstract class AnimalFactory
```

```
{
    // Deferring the instantiation process
    // to the subclasses.
    public abstract IAnimal CreateAnimal();
}
/// <summary>
/// CatFactory creates cats.
/// </summary>
class CatFactory : AnimalFactory
{
    public override IAnimal CreateAnimal()
    {
        return new Cat();
    }
}
/// <summary>
/// TigerFactory creates tigers.
/// </summary>
class TigerFactory : AnimalFactory
{
    public override IAnimal CreateAnimal()
    {
        return new Tiger();
    }
}
#endregion
```

Why is this helpful? In the upcoming demonstration, you'll see that I use this construct in a way that the entire code segment is closed for modification. In the future, if you need to support a new animal type, say, a monkey, you need to do the following:

- Create a Monkey class that will implement the IAnimal interface

- Create a MonkeyFactory that will implement the AnimalFactory and provide the implementation for the CreateAnimal() method

So, it is enough for you to test the new classes only. *Your existing code is untouched, and it is closed for modification*.

Before you see the complete demonstration, I want you to note these two separate inheritance hierarchies, where one is for the animal hierarchy and another one is for the factory hierarchy. I have marked them inside this code for your ready reference. I also include Figure 6-1 for better clarity.

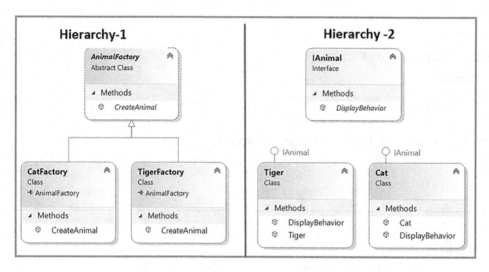

Figure 6-1. *The class diagram shows the two different hierarchies in demonstration 2*

Demonstration 2

Here is the complete demonstration:

```
Console.WriteLine("***Modified version of demonstration 1. ***");
// The CatFactory creates cats
AnimalFactory animalFactory = new CatFactory();
IAnimal animal = animalFactory.CreateAnimal();
animal.DisplayBehavior();

// The TigerFactory creates tigers
animalFactory = new TigerFactory();
animal = animalFactory.CreateAnimal();
animal.DisplayBehavior();

#region Animal hierarchy
```

```csharp
interface IAnimal
{
    void DisplayBehavior();
}

class Tiger : IAnimal
{
    public Tiger()
    {
        Console.WriteLine("\nA tiger is created.");
    }
    public void DisplayBehavior()
    {
        Console.WriteLine("""
        It roars.
        It loves to roam in the jungle.
        """);
    }
}

class Cat : IAnimal
{
    public Cat()
    {
        Console.WriteLine("\nA cat is created.");
    }
    public void DisplayBehavior()
    {
        Console.WriteLine("""
        It meows.
        It loves to stay at a home.
        """);
    }
}
#endregion

#region Factory hierarchy
```

```csharp
/// <summary>
/// This class contains the "factory method"
/// </summary>
abstract class AnimalFactory
{
    // Deferring the instantiation process
    // to the subclasses.
    public abstract IAnimal CreateAnimal();
}

/// <summary>
/// CatFactory creates cats.
/// </summary>
class CatFactory : AnimalFactory
{
    public override IAnimal CreateAnimal()
    {
        return new Cat();
    }
}

/// <summary>
/// TigerFactory creates tigers.
/// </summary>
class TigerFactory : AnimalFactory
{
    public override IAnimal CreateAnimal()
    {
        return new Tiger();
    }
}
#endregion
```

Output

Except for the first line, this output is the same as the previous output:

```
***Modified version of demonstration 1. ***

A cat is created.
It meows.
It loves to stay at a home.

A tiger is created.
It roars.
It loves to roam in the jungle.
```

Analysis

We can summarize this modified implementation with the following points:

- Inside the client code, you decide which animal factory to use, a CatFactory or a TigerFactory.

- The subclasses of AnimalFactory create a Cat instance or a Tiger instance.

- Following this, we are supporting the OCP. As a result, it is a better and more extensible solution.

A New Requirement

In Chapter 4, I said that it is not always easy to fully implement this principle, but partial OCP compliance too can generate greater benefits for you. A new requirement can demand many changes in an application. In such a case, based on the situation, you have to choose one technique over another.

In the previous demonstrations, each factory could produce only one type of object, either a cat or a tiger, but there is no variation. For example, it makes perfect sense if a cat factory makes cats of different colors. Similarly, a tiger factory can produce tigers of different colors. If you receive such a requirement, how can you proceed? One option is to pass a color attribute inside the constructor and update the program accordingly.

The following is a sample demonstration for this. I have highlighted the important changes in bold.

Demonstration 3

Here is the complete implementation:

```
Console.WriteLine("***Modifying demonstration 2
  now. ***");
// The CatFactory creates cats
AnimalFactory animalFactory = new CatFactory();
IAnimal animal = animalFactory.CreateAnimal("black");
animal.DisplayBehavior();

// The TigerFactory creates tigers
animalFactory = new TigerFactory();
animal = animalFactory.CreateAnimal("white");
animal.DisplayBehavior();

#region Animal hierarchy
interface IAnimal
{
    void DisplayBehavior();
}
class Tiger : IAnimal
{
    public Tiger(string color)
    {
        Console.WriteLine($"\nA {color} tiger is created.");
    }

    public void DisplayBehavior()
    {
        Console.WriteLine("""
        It roars.
        It loves to roam in the jungle.
```

```csharp
            """);
        }
}
class Cat : IAnimal
{
    public Cat(string color)
    {
        Console.WriteLine($"\nA {color} cat is created.");
    }

    public void DisplayBehavior()
    {
        Console.WriteLine("""
          It meows.
          It loves to stay at a home.
          """);
    }
}
#endregion

#region Factory hierarchy
abstract class AnimalFactory
{
    public abstract IAnimal CreateAnimal(string color);
}
class CatFactory : AnimalFactory
{
    public override IAnimal CreateAnimal(string color)
    {
        return new Cat(color);
    }
}
class TigerFactory : AnimalFactory
{
```

```
    public override IAnimal CreateAnimal(string color)
    {
        return new Tiger(color);
    }
}
#endregion
```

Output

This program produces the following output:

```
***Modifying demonstration 2 now. ***

A black cat is created.
It meows.
It loves to stay at a home.

A white tiger is created.
It roars.
It loves to roam in the jungle.
```

Analysis

You can see that lots of changes are required in this case. Is there any alternative way? I think so. This is why I have made demonstration 4 for you.

Since AnimalFactory is an abstract class, you can modify this class too to accommodate this change. In this alternative demonstration, I introduce a new method, MakeAnimal(), which accepts the color attribute before it calls the CreateAnimal() method to make an animal instance. Here is the code:

```
abstract class AnimalFactory
{
    public IAnimal MakeAnimal(string color)
    {
        Console.WriteLine($"\nThe following animal
          color is {color}.");
        IAnimal animal= CreateAnimal();
```

```
            return animal;
        }
        public abstract IAnimal CreateAnimal();
    }
```

In the client code, you call the MakeAnimal() method instead of CreateAnimal() to see the effect of the updated code. Demonstration 4 shows you the complete example.

Demonstration 4

Here is the complete implementation:

```
Console.WriteLine("***Modifying demonstration 2 (an
  alternative approach).***");
// The CatFactory creates cats
AnimalFactory animalFactory = new CatFactory();
IAnimal animal = animalFactory.MakeAnimal("black");
animal.DisplayBehavior();

// The TigerFactory creates tigers
animalFactory = new TigerFactory();
animal = animalFactory.MakeAnimal("white");
animal.DisplayBehavior();

#region Animal hierarchy

interface IAnimal
{
    void DisplayBehavior();
}
class Tiger : Ianimal
{
    public Tiger()
    {
        Console.WriteLine("A tiger is created.");
    }
    public void DisplayBehavior()
    {
```

```csharp
        Console.WriteLine("""
        It roars.
        It loves to roam in the jungle.
        """);
    }
}
class Cat : Ianimal
{
    public Cat()
    {
        Console.WriteLine("A cat is created.");
    }
    public void DisplayBehavior()
    {
        Console.WriteLine("""
        It meows.
        It loves to stay at a home.
        """);
    }
}
#endregion

#region Factory hierarchy

abstract class AnimalFactory
{
    public Ianimal MakeAnimal(string color)
    {
        Console.WriteLine($"\nThe following animal
          color is {color}.");
        IAnimal animal = CreateAnimal();
        return animal;
    }
    public abstract IAnimal CreateAnimal();
}
class CatFactory : AnimalFactory
```

```
{
    public override IAnimal CreateAnimal()
    {
        return new Cat();
    }
}
class TigerFactory : AnimalFactory
{
    public override IAnimal CreateAnimal()
    {
        return new Tiger();
    }
}
#endregion
```

Output

Here is the output:

```
***Modifying demonstration 2 (an alternative approach).***
```

The following animal color is black.
```
A cat is created.
It meows.
It loves to stay at a home.
```

The following animal color is white.
```
A tiger is created.
It roars.
It loves to roam in the jungle.
```

Summary

Factories provide an alternative way to create objects. In this chapter, you saw the advantage of using factories. This chapter started with a simple factory class, which helps you to separate the code that is likely to vary from the other parts of the code. You put the instantiation logic inside the factory class to provide a uniform way to create objects.

Following the OCP principle, you further modified the application. In demonstration 2, you used a new hierarchy for factories where all concrete factories inherit from AnimalFactory, and you passed the details of object creation to a concrete factory (CatFactory or TigerFactory). Since you are following the OCP principle, you can add a new concrete factory, say MonkeyFactory, to create monkeys. And when you consider this scenario, you do not need to reopen the existing code. Instead, the new MonkeyFactory class can inherit from AnimalFactory, and following the rules, it can create monkeys. In this case, you need to create a Monkey class using the same approach I used for the Tiger class or the Cat class. Notice that you do not need to reopen the existing code.

I created demonstration 3 and demonstration 4 to support a new requirement. Maintaining the OCP in the current structure to accommodate the new requirement was tough because the color attribute was not considered at the beginning. In demonstration 3, you saw the use of a **parameterized factory** method to accommodate a new requirement. Finally, in demonstration 4, you saw that inside the abstract factory class, you can set a common rule that all derived concrete factories must follow. This approach helped you accommodate the particular change requirement with minimum changes.

CHAPTER 7

Add Features Using Wrappers

An alternative to inheritance is composition. It is quite common in programming and often gives you a better payoff. This chapter shows you a useful case study on this topic using some wrappers.

The first question that may come into your mind is, what is a wrapper? *A wrapper is like a topping that surrounds an object. In programming, you often use a wrapper to add some functionalities dynamically.* This is a powerful technique because you can add or discard a wrapper as per your needs, and it does not hamper the functionalities of the original object.

Say you need to work on a piece of code and add some new features. Someone coded it before you, and you cannot change the existing code. This scenario is common in software industries when you need to enhance a feature to attract new customers but you cannot alter the existing workflow of the software to support the existing customers. You understand that in this case, since you were not a part of the team that wrote the first version of the software, you do not have exclusive control of it. Wrappers are useful in similar situations. As mentioned, in this case, you can add new functionality on top of the existing functionality to support new customers. In fact, by using different types of wrappers, you can attract different types of customers too. The upcoming example will make the concept clearer to you.

© Vaskaran Sarcar 2023
V. Sarcar, *Simple and Efficient Programming with C#*, https://doi.org/10.1007/978-1-4842-8737-8_7

The Problem Statement

Assume that several people want to purchase a property. The budget and mindset of every individual are different. These people visit a home builder to get a cost estimate. For simplicity, let's assume that the people have the following options:

- Either they can build a basic home with minimum facilities or they can build an advanced home with more facilities. For illustration purposes, we'll refer to these homes as the BasicHome and AdvancedHome, respectively.

- The home builder gives them options; a customer can opt for a playground, a swimming pool, or both. Let's call these *luxuries*. Each of these luxuries has additional costs for a buyer.

Based on the budget restrictions, a customer can opt for various options, and the final price will vary. Most important, a customer who opts for a BasicHome today can upgrade their home tomorrow by adding one playground or a swimming pool (or both). Can you write a program for this scenario?

Initial Program (Using Subclassing)

If you try to provide a solution using inheritance, first try to understand the associated problems. Activities like this will give you a better payoff in the long run. Let us start with the following demonstration.

Demonstration 1

Assume that you have started with the following code:

```
class Home
{
    // Some code
}
class Playground : Home
{
    // Some code
}
```

```
class SwimmingPool : Playground
{
    // Some code
}
```

This is not a recommended approach, because to get a swimming pool, you first get a playground, which a customer may not want. Because of similar logic, the following structure is not a good choice either:

```
class Home
{
    // Some code
}
Class SwimmingPool : Home
{
    // Some code
}
class Playground : SwimmingPool
{
    // Some code
}
```

This is because this time to get a playground you first get a swimming pool, which a customer may not want. ***So, implementing a multilevel inheritance, in this case, is not a good idea!***

Now let's assume that you start with a hierarchical inheritance where SwimmingPool and Playground both inherit from the Home class, as shown in Figure 7-1.

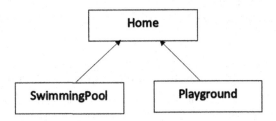

Figure 7-1. *A hierarchical inheritance*

Now you need a home with a swimming pool and a playground. So, you end up with the design shown in Figure 7-2.

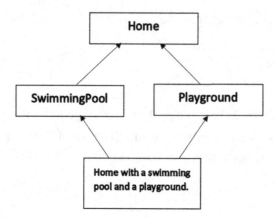

Figure 7-2. *A class needs to inherit from multiple base classes. It causes the diamond problem in C#*

But you know that ***you cannot have multiple base classes in C#.*** So, any construct like the following will raise a compilation error too:

```
class Home: SwimmingPool, Playground // Error
{

}
```

Now you understand that simple subclassing, in this case, is not a good idea. What are the alternatives? Let's continue investigating.

You may proceed with an interface for the luxury items. For example, you can opt for the following interface:

```
interface ILuxury
{
    void AddPlayground();
    void AddSwimmingPool();
}
```

Now you can have a class that can implement this interface. For example, here is a Home class that extends the BasicHome class and implements the ILuxury interface:

```
class Home : BasicHome, ILuxury
{
    public void AddPlayground()
    {
```

```
        // Some code
    }

    public void AddSwimmingPool()
    {
        // Some code
    }
}
```

But again, a customer may opt for a home with one of these luxuries but not both. In that case, if a method is not needed, you write this:

```
throw new NotImplementedException();
```

The problem associated with this is discussed in the context of the LSP in Chapter 4. To avoid this, you may follow the ISP and segregate the ILuxury interface. Yes, this time it can work! Since you saw a similar solution in Chapter 2, I won't repeat it here.

Now we will look at an alternative approach.

Better Program (Using Object Composition)

Let's see how a wrapper can help you. ***Using a wrapper, you surround an object with another object.*** The enclosing object is often called a ***decorator***, which conforms to the interface of the component that it decorates. It forwards the requests to the original component and can perform additional operations before or after those requests. ***You can add an unlimited number of responsibilities with this concept.*** The following figures help you understand this.

Figure 7-3 shows that the home (basic or advanced) is surrounded by a playground.

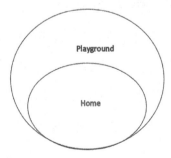

Figure 7-3. *The home is surrounded by a playground*

155

Figure 7-4 shows the home that is surrounded by a swimming pool.

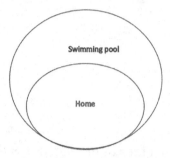

Figure 7-4. *The home is surrounded by a swimming pool*

Figure 7-5 shows the home that is surrounded by a playground and a swimming pool. Here you first surround the home with a playground, and then you surround the structure with a swimming pool.

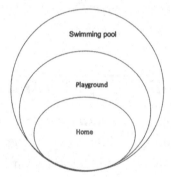

Figure 7-5. *The home is surrounded by a playground and a swimming pool*

Figure 7-6 shows the home that is surrounded by a swimming pool and a playground again. But this time you change the order; you first surround the home with a swimming pool, and then you surround it with a playground.

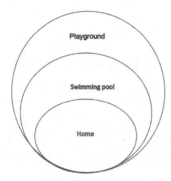

Figure 7-6. *The home is surrounded by a swimming pool. Later you surround the structure with a playground*

Note   Following this same technique, you can add two more playgrounds or swimming pools.

Let's try to implement this concept following the requirements we have.

In the upcoming demonstration, six players are involved. Let's call them Home, BasicHome, AdvancedHome, Luxury, Playground, and SwimmingPool.

The Home is defined as follows:

```
abstract class Home
    {
        public double basePrice = 100000;
        public double AdditionalCost { get; set; }
        public abstract void BuildHome();
        public virtual double GetPrice()
        {
            return basePrice + AdditionalCost;
        }
    }
```

Here are some important points before you read further:

- You can see that a concrete implementor of Home must implement the BuildHome() method. If needed, it can override the GetPrice() method too. In this example, BasicHome and AdvancedHome inherit from Home.

- I assume that the base price of a home is $100,000. Using the AdditionalCost property, one can set some extra prices. I use this property to set an additional cost for an advanced home. Currently, for a basic home, this cost is 0, and for an advanced home, this cost is $25000.

- I assume that once the home is built, there is no need for an immediate modification. One can add the luxuries later.

- Once a home is built, you can opt for a playground or a swimming pool for an existing home, or you may want both. So, the Playground and SwimmingPool classes appear in this example.

- Though it was not strictly needed, to share the common code, both the Playground class and the SwimmingPool class inherit from the abstract class Luxury, which has the following structure:

```
abstract class Luxury : Home
{
  protected Home home;
  public double LuxuryCost { get; set; }
   public Luxury(Home home)
   {
      this.home = home;
   }
   public override void BuildHome()
   {
      home.BuildHome();
   }
}
```

- Like the AdditionalCost property, one can set (or update) a luxury cost using the LuxuryCost property.

- Notice that Luxury holds a reference for Home and the concrete decorators (Playground or SwimmingPool in this example) are decorating an instance of Home.

- Now let's look into the structure of a concrete decorator, say, Playground, which is as follows:

```
class Playground : Luxury
{
    public Playground(Home home) : base(home)
    {
        this.LuxuryCost = 20000;
    }
    public override void BuildHome()
    {
        base.BuildHome();
        AddPlayground();
    }

    private void AddPlayground()
    {
      Console.WriteLine($"""
        For a playground, you pay an extra
         ${this.LuxuryCost}.
        Now the total cost is ${GetPrice()}.
        """);
    }
    public override double GetPrice()
    {
        return home.GetPrice() + LuxuryCost;
    }
}
```

- You can see that using the AddPlayground() method, you can add a playground. When you avail of this facility, you have to pay an additional $20,000. I initialize this value inside the constructor. Most important, notice that before adding a playground, it calls BuildHome() from the base class Luxury. This method in turn calls the BuildHome() from a concrete implementation of Home.

- The SwimmingPool class works similarly, but you have to pay more for this. (Yes, I assume that a swimming pool costs more than a playground in this case.)

Class Diagram

Figure 7-7 shows the most important parts of the class diagram.

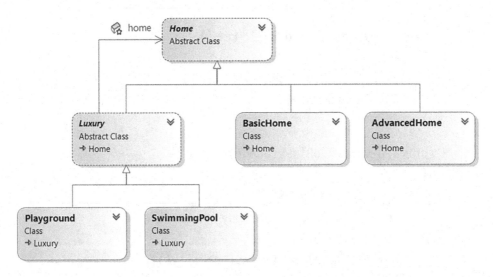

Figure 7-7. *The class diagram shows the key participants in demonstration 1*

Demonstration 2

Here is the complete demonstration for you. In the client code, you can see many different scenarios to show the effectiveness of this application.

```
Console.WriteLine("***Using wrappers.***");
Console.WriteLine("Scenario-1: A basic home with basic facilities.");
Home home = new BasicHome();
home.BuildHome();

Console.WriteLine("\nScenario-2: A basic home with an
 additional playground.");
Luxury homeWithOnePlayground = new Playground(home);
homeWithOnePlayground.BuildHome();

Console.WriteLine("\nScenario-3: A basic home with two
 additional playgrounds.");
Luxury homeWithDoublePlaygrounds = new Playground(homeWithOnePlayground);
homeWithDoublePlaygrounds.BuildHome();

Console.WriteLine("\nScenario-4: A basic home with one
 additional playground and swimming pool.");
Luxury homeWithOnePlaygroundAndOneSwimmingPool = new SwimmingPool(homeWith
 OnePlayground);
homeWithOnePlaygroundAndOneSwimmingPool.BuildHome();

Console.WriteLine("\nScenario-5: Adding a swimming
 pool and then a playground to a basic home.");
Luxury homeWithOneSwimmingPool = new SwimmingPool(home);
Luxury homeWithSwimmingPoolAndPlayground = new Playground(homeWithOne
 SwimmingPool);
homeWithSwimmingPoolAndPlayground.BuildHome();

Console.WriteLine("\nScenario-6: An advanced home with
 some more facilities.");
home = new AdvancedHome();
home.BuildHome();

Console.WriteLine("\nScenario-7: An advanced home with
 an additional playground.");
homeWithOnePlayground = new Playground(home);
homeWithOnePlayground.BuildHome();
```

```csharp
abstract class Home
{
    public double basePrice = 100000;
    public double AdditionalCost { get; set; }
    public abstract void BuildHome();
    public virtual double GetPrice()
    {
        return basePrice + AdditionalCost;
    }
}
class BasicHome : Home
{
    public BasicHome()
    {
        AdditionalCost = 0;
    }
    public override void BuildHome()
    {
        Console.WriteLine($"""
          A home with basic facilities is made.
          It costs ${GetPrice()}.
          """);
    }
}

class AdvancedHome : Home
{
    public AdvancedHome()
    {
        AdditionalCost = 25000;
    }
    public override void BuildHome()
    {
        Console.WriteLine($"""
          A home with advanced facilities is made.
          It costs ${GetPrice()}.
```

```csharp
            """);
    }
}
abstract class Luxury : Home
{
    protected Home home;
    public double LuxuryCost { get; set; }
    public Luxury(Home home)
    {
        this.home = home;
    }
    public override void BuildHome()
    {
        home.BuildHome();
    }
}
class Playground : Luxury
{
    public Playground(Home home) : base(home)
    {
        this.LuxuryCost = 20000;
    }
    public override void BuildHome()
    {
        base.BuildHome();
        AddPlayground();
    }

    private void AddPlayground()
    {
        Console.WriteLine($"""
          For a playground, you pay an extra
           ${this.LuxuryCost}.
          Now the total cost is ${GetPrice()}.
          """);
    }
```

```csharp
    public override double GetPrice()
    {
        return home.GetPrice() + LuxuryCost;
    }
}

class SwimmingPool : Luxury
{
    public SwimmingPool(Home home) : base(home)
    {
        this.LuxuryCost = 55000;
    }
    public override void BuildHome()
    {
        base.BuildHome();
        AddSwimmingPool();
    }

    private void AddSwimmingPool()
    {
        Console.WriteLine($"""
          For a swimming pool, you pay an extra
           ${this.LuxuryCost}.
          Now the total cost is ${GetPrice()}.
          """);
    }
    public override double GetPrice()
    {
        return home.GetPrice() + LuxuryCost;
    }
}
```

Output

Here is the output. I have highlighted different scenarios in bold font for your reference.

```
***Using wrappers.***
```

Scenario-1: A basic home with basic facilities.
```
A home with basic facilities is made.
It costs $100000.
```

Scenario-2: A basic home with an additional playground.
```
A home with basic facilities is made.
It costs $100000.
For a playground, you pay an extra $20000.
Now the total cost is $120000.
```

Scenario-3: A basic home with two additional playgrounds.
```
A home with basic facilities is made.
It costs $100000.
For a playground, you pay an extra $20000.
Now the total cost is $120000.
For a playground, you pay an extra $20000.
Now the total cost is $140000.
```

Scenario-4: A basic home with one additional playground and swimming pool.
```
A home with basic facilities is made.
It costs $100000.
For a playground, you pay an extra $20000.
Now the total cost is $120000.
For a swimming pool, you pay an extra $55000.
Now the total cost is $175000.
```

Scenario-5: Adding a swimming pool and then a playground to the basic home.
```
A home with basic facilities is made.
It costs $100000.
For a swimming pool, you pay an extra $55000.
Now the total cost is $155000.
For a playground, you pay an extra $20000.
Now the total cost is $175000.
```

Scenario-6: An advanced home with some more facilities.
A home with advanced facilities is made.
It costs $125000.

Scenario-7: An advanced home with an additional playground.
A home with advanced facilities is made.
It costs $125000.
For a playground, you pay an extra $20000.
Now the total cost is $145000.

Analysis

Notice that this implementation follows the OCP principle. So, when you make a different type of home, you do not need to open the existing code; instead, you can make a new class that inherits from the abstract class Home.

I want you to note that I slightly violated the SRP in this example. This is because I wanted to show you the final price after uniformly adding a luxury. In actuality, when I add a wrapper, I do not need to calculate the total cost; instead, it is sufficient to show the increased price for this addition. But I assume that a customer would like to see the total estimated price. This is the reason, after each addition of a luxury item, I showed the total cost. In addition, the price depends on the type of home you choose. So, it makes sense to put the GetPrice() method and the BuildHome() method in the Home class.

This example pattern is more effective when you use a wrapper that does a single job. So, when you follow the SRP, you can add or remove a behavior easily using this kind of wrapper.

I am about to finish this chapter. Before that, I want to inform you that when you analyze I/O stream implementations in the .NET Framework and Java, you will find many similar implementations. For example, the BufferedStream class inherits from the abstract base class Stream. I am taking a snapshot from the Visual Studio IDE to show you the constructors of this class (see Figure 7-8).

```
...public sealed class BufferedStream : Stream
{
    ...public BufferedStream(Stream stream);
    ...public BufferedStream(Stream stream, int bufferSize);
```

Figure 7-8. *Partial snapshot of BufferedStream class from the Visual Studio IDE*

You can see that the BufferedStream class constructors accept a Steam class object as a parameter. Notice that the Luxury constructor also accepts its base class object (Home) as a parameter. So, you can say that the Luxury and BufferedStream classes follow the wrapper/decorator pattern.

But now notice the partial snapshot of the FileStream class from the Visual Studio IDE (see Figure 7-9).

```
...public class FileStream : Stream
{
    ...public FileStream(SafeFileHandle handle, FileAccess access);
    ...public FileStream(IntPtr handle, FileAccess access);
    ...public FileStream(string path, FileMode mode);
    ...public FileStream(string path, FileStreamOptions options);
    ...public FileStream(SafeFileHandle handle, FileAccess access, int bufferSize);
    ...public FileStream(IntPtr handle, FileAccess access, bool ownsHandle);
    ...public FileStream(string path, FileMode mode, FileAccess access);
    ...public FileStream(SafeFileHandle handle, FileAccess access, int bufferSize, bool isAsync);
    ...public FileStream(IntPtr handle, FileAccess access, bool ownsHandle, int bufferSize);
    ...public FileStream(string path, FileMode mode, FileAccess access, FileShare share);
    ...public FileStream(IntPtr handle, FileAccess access, bool ownsHandle, int bufferSize, bool isAsync);
    ...public FileStream(string path, FileMode mode, FileAccess access, FileShare share, int bufferSize);
    ...public FileStream(string path, FileMode mode, FileAccess access, FileShare share, int bufferSize, bool useAsync);
    ...public FileStream(string path, FileMode mode, FileAccess access, FileShare share, int bufferSize, FileOptions options);
```

Figure 7-9. *Partial snapshot of the FileStream class from the Visual Studio 2022 IDE*

You can see that there is no constructor of the FileStream class that can accept a Steam class object as a parameter. So, this class does not follow the wrapper/decorator pattern.

Summary

The pattern that is shown in this chapter is referred to as a *wrapper* or a *decorator pattern*. This chapter shows you an alternative way to implement the subclassing technique. You have seen the reason why neither the multilevel inheritance nor the multiple inheritance can solve the problem that we mentioned at the beginning of the chapter. Later you saw an implementation using object composition. You used different types of wrappers to add a behavior dynamically in this application. In this context, you can remember that a simple inheritance promotes only a compile-time binding, not a dynamic binding.

In short, here are the key points that you learned in this chapter:

- You can add a state and/or behavior without modifying an existing inheritance hierarchy.

- In demonstration 2, you defined a new hierarchy that itself extends the root of the original/existing hierarchy.

- To use the decorators, you first instantiate a home and then wrap it inside a decorator.

- This example pattern has a name. We call it the **decorator pattern**. It shows an example of when object composition can perform better than plain inheritance.

- You also saw some built-in examples in .NET. There you learned that the BufferedStream class follows a similar pattern, but the FileStream class does not follow this pattern.

CHAPTER 8

Make Efficient Templates Using Hooks

This chapter will show you two important techniques. First, you will learn to use a template method. Why is this important? It is important because template methods are one of the fundamental techniques for code reuse. Suppose you follow a multistep algorithm to achieve a task. Using a template method, you can redefine some of these steps (but not all the steps) of the algorithm without altering the calling sequence of these steps.

This chapter starts with a demonstration that uses a template method. In addition, you'll use a hook method to enhance this application.

The Problem Statement

A dealer (or seller) can sell various products such as televisions, washing machines, or music players. Assume that you know such a dealer. You can visit a showroom to purchase a television. You can visit the same showroom to purchase a washing machine for your home. In each case, you can summarize the overall activity in the following order:

1. You visit the dealer showroom.
2. You purchase a product.
3. The dealer generates a bill for you.
4. The dealer delivers the product to you.

Can you make an application that mimics this scenario?

169

© Vaskaran Sarcar 2023
V. Sarcar, *Simple and Efficient Programming with C#*, https://doi.org/10.1007/978-1-4842-8737-8_8

Initial Program

In the upcoming program, I assume that you purchase a washing machine and a television from the same dealer. When you purchase a television, you see the following output:

1. The customer visits a dealer showroom.
2. The customer purchases a television.
3. The bill is printed.
4. The product is delivered.

When you purchase a washing machine, you see the following output:

1. The customer visits a dealer showroom.
2. The customer purchases a washing machine.
3. The bill is printed.
4. The product is delivered.

Notice that step 1, step 3, and step 4 are common in both cases. You do not see any difference in these steps when you purchase different products. Also notice that these steps are fixed. For example, once you purchase a product, then the bill is generated, and the product is delivered. It is unlikely the dealer will generate a bill and deliver the product if you do not visit the showroom or choose the product. (I do not consider online shopping in this case.)

Designing a template method is ideal in this scenario where you do not alter the basic steps of an algorithm, but you allow some minor modifications in some steps. In our example, step 2 changes slightly to show the product you select, but the remaining steps are the same when you buy any product.

When you order a pizza, you notice a similar scenario. For example, you can opt for different toppings such as bacon, onions, extra cheese, or mushrooms for a pizza. How does the chef make the pizza? The chef first prepares the pizza following conventional ways. Just before delivery, the chef can include the toppings to make you happy. You can find similar situations in other domains too.

Now the question is, how can you make such an application that has multiple steps but only a few of them can vary? Obviously, you can use different approaches, but the simple answer is that you can use a template method (that consists of many steps) in a parent class. Then you defer some steps to the subclasses (that represent the particular product) and allow derived classes to override those steps based on their needs.

Note   Using simple polymorphism, you can bring a radical change by overriding all, or most, of the methods of a parent class inside a child class. By contrast, when you use a template method, you do not override all the parent class (or, base class) methods in the child class. Instead, you override only a limited number of methods (or, steps). This is the key distinction between this approach and simple polymorphism.

In the upcoming example, you can see the following class that contains a template method called PurchaseProduct. The overall code is simple; still, I have kept the comments in the code to help you understand it.

```
public abstract class Device
{
  // The following method(step) will NOT vary
  private void VisitShowroom()
  {
   Console.WriteLine("1. The customer visits a dealer showroom.");
  }
// The following method(step) will NOT vary
private void GenerateBill()
{
  Console.WriteLine("3. The bill is printed.");
}
private void DeliverProduct()
{
  Console.WriteLine("4. The product is delivered. \n");
}
/*
The following method will vary. It will be
overridden by derived classes.
*/
protected abstract void SelectProduct();
// The template method
```

```
public void PurchaseProduct()
{
  // Step-1
  VisitShowroom();
  // Step-2: Specialized action
  SelectProduct();
  // Step-3
  GenerateBill();
  // Step-4
  DeliverProduct();
  }
}
```

Here are the important points:

- This class is abstract because it contains the abstract method SelectProduct(). A child class of this class overrides this method to show the product you purchased.

- Inside the template method you see four methods: VisitShowroom(), SelectProduct(), GenerateBill(), and DeliverProduct(). *These four methods represent the four steps of the algorithm.*

- SelectProduct() is a **protected** method. It allows a derived class to redefine/override the method. But the other methods inside the template method are marked with the **private** keyword/access modifier. So, a client cannot access them directly.

- When you call the PurchaseProduct() method, a derived class cannot alter the execution order of these methods. Also inside the client code, you cannot access these methods directly. To complete a purchase, you need to invoke the template method. This is why I made this template method public. Clients do not know how the template method accomplishes its task. Since you do not expose the inner logic to a client, this is a better practice.

Note   The participating classes are small. So, similar to other programs in this book, instead of creating separate files (or, namespaces), I have put them together in a single file.

Class Diagram

Figure 8-1 shows the important parts of the class diagram.

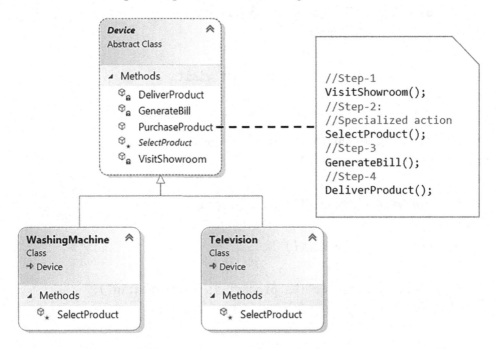

Figure 8-1.   *PurchaseProduct() is the template method in this example.*

Demonstration 1

Here is the complete demonstration:

```
Console.WriteLine("***A demonstration of a template Method.***\n");
Console.WriteLine("---The customer wants a television.---");
Device device = new Television();
device.PurchaseProduct();
```

```
Console.WriteLine("---The customer wants a washing machine.---");
device = new WashingMachine();
device.PurchaseProduct();

/// <summary>
/// Basic skeleton of action steps
/// </summary>
public abstract class Device
{

    // The following method(step) will NOT vary
    private void VisitShowroom()
    {
        Console.WriteLine("1. The customer visits a
          dealer showroom.");
    }
    // The following method(step) will NOT vary
    private void GenerateBill()
    {
        Console.WriteLine("3. The bill is printed.");
    }
    private void DeliverProduct()
    {
        Console.WriteLine("4. The product is delivered.\n");
    }
    /*
    The following method will vary. It will be
    overridden by derived classes.
    */

    protected abstract void SelectProduct();

    // The template method
    public void PurchaseProduct()
    {
        // Step-1
        VisitShowroom();
        // Step-2: Specialized action
```

```csharp
        SelectProduct();
        // Step-3
        GenerateBill();
        // Step-4
        DeliverProduct();
    }
}

// The concrete derived class:Television
public class Television : Device
{
    protected override void SelectProduct()
    {
        Console.WriteLine("2. The customer purchases a
            television.");
    }
}

// The concrete derived class:WashingMachine
public class WashingMachine : Device
{
    protected override void SelectProduct()
    {
        Console.WriteLine("2. The customer purchases a
            washing machine.");
    }
}
```

Output

Here is the output:

```
***A demonstration of a template Method.***

---The customer wants a television.---
1. The customer visits a dealer showroom.
2. The customer purchases a television.
```

3. The bill is printed.

4. The product is delivered.

```
---The customer wants a washing machine.---
```
1. The customer visits a dealer showroom.

2. The customer purchases a washing machine.

3. The bill is printed.

4. The product is delivered.

Analysis

In the future if you need to consider a different product, say a DVD, you can easily enhance the application. In that case, you can create a DVD class that inherits from `Device` and overrides the `SelectProduct()` method in the same way. Here is a sample for you:

```
// The concrete derived class:DVD
public class DVD : Device
{
    protected override void SelectProduct()
    {
        Console.WriteLine("2. The customer
            purchases a DVD player.");
    }
}
```

Note   This implementation obeys the OCP principle. But does this implementation violate the SRP? The answer seems to be yes to some extent. But think from a seller's perspective: a potential customer visits the showroom and selects the product. Then the seller generates the bill and delivers the product to the customer. All these activities are linked to "one successful sell" from a seller's point of view. From this perspective, you spread out these steps to accomplish one single task, which is purchasing a product. This is why a customer in this example can access only the template method, and other methods are private to the customer. In addition, you may recall what I said in the preface: sometimes it is OK to bend a rule based on the complexity or nature of a problem.

Enhanced Requirement

Let's enhance the application and consider another real-world scenario. The dealer can decide to offer a special gift coupon to a customer who purchases a television from him. This offer does not apply to other products. How can you modify this application to serve this new requirement?

One approach is straightforward. You use a method (it can be public or protected) to reflect this offer and place the method inside the parent class Device. Let's name this method GenerateGiftCoupon(). It is introduced in the following code segment and shown in bold:

```
/// <summary>
/// Basic skeleton of action steps
/// </summary>
public abstract class Device
{

    // The following method(step) will NOT vary
    private void VisitShowroom()
    {
    Console.WriteLine("1.The customer visits a dealer showroom.");
    }
    // The following method(step) will NOT vary
    private void GenerateBill()
    {
    Console.WriteLine("3.The bill is printed.");
    }
    private void DeliverProduct()
    {
    Console.WriteLine("4.The product is delivered.\n");
    }
    /*
    The following method will vary. It will be
    overridden by derived classes.
    */
    protected abstract void SelectProduct();
```

```
// The template method
public void PurchaseProduct()
{
    // Step-1
    VisitShowroom();
    // Step-2: Specialized action
    SelectProduct();
    // Step-2.1: Eligible for a gift?
    GenerateGiftCoupon();
    // Step-3
    GenerateBill();
    // Step-4
    DeliverProduct();
}
protected virtual void GenerateGiftCoupon()
{
 Console.WriteLine("\tA gift coupon is generated.");
}
}
```

Now any subclass of Device can have the GenerateGiftCoupon() method. Each subclass can redefine it as per their own needs. Per our new requirements, you get a special gift coupon from the dealer if you purchase a television, but not for a washing machine. So, inside the WashingMachine class, you override the method and write it in the following way:

```
protected override void GenerateGiftCoupon()
{
  throw new NotImplementedException();
}
```

But throwing an exception inside a method body can be risky in certain scenarios. You learned about this when I discussed the LSP in Chapter 4.

To avoid this problem, you can make this method empty as follows:

```
protected override void GenerateGiftCoupon()
 {
  // Empty body
 }
```

Now, is it a good idea to use an empty method? I think we can find a better alternative.

You may want to make GenerateGiftCoupon() abstract and override it in its child classes as per their needs. Yes, this will work. But the problem is that when you use an abstract method in the parent class, the derived classes need to provide a concrete implementation for the method (otherwise, it is again abstract, and you cannot instantiate from it). *So, if you have too many specialized classes and most of them don't make you eligible for gift coupons, you are still forced to override them.* (Remember the ISP?)

Is there a better solution? Yes, I think so. You can use a hook method. I am about to show this in demonstration 2. Before you proceed, the question is, *what is a hook in programming? In very simple words, a hook helps you execute some code before or after an existing code. It can help you extend the behavior of a program at runtime. Hook methods can provide some default behaviors that a subclass can override if necessary. Often, they do nothing by default.*

Let me show you the use of a simple hook in this program. Notice the bold lines in the following code segments:

```
// The template method
public void PurchaseProduct()
{
    // Step-1
    VisitShowroom();
    //Step-2: Specialized action
    SelectProduct();
    // Step-2.1: Eligible for a gift?
    if(IsEligibleForGiftCoupon())
    {
        GenerateGiftCoupon();
    }
```

```
        // Step-3
        GenerateBill();
        // Step-4
        DeliverProduct();
    }
```

The hook method is defined as follows:

```
// By default, there is no gift coupon.
protected virtual bool IsEligibleForGiftCoupon()
{
  return false;
}
```

These two code segments tell us that when you invoke the template method, by default GenerateGiftCoupon() will not be executed. This is because IsEligibleForGiftCoupon() returns false, which in turn makes the if condition inside the template method false. But the Television class overrides this method as follows:

```
protected override bool IsEligibleForGiftCoupon()
{
  return true;
}
```

So, when you instantiate a Television object and call the template method, you can see that GenerateGiftCoupon() is called just before step 3.

Demonstration 2

Here is the complete demonstration using a hook method. I kept the comments in the code.

```
Console.WriteLine("***A demonstration of a template Method.***\n");
Console.WriteLine("---The customer wants a television.----");
Device device = new Television();
device.PurchaseProduct();

Console.WriteLine("---The customer wants a washing machine.---");
device = new WashingMachine();
device.PurchaseProduct();
```

```csharp
/// <summary>
/// Basic skeleton of action steps
/// </summary>
public abstract class Device
{

    // The following method(step) will NOT vary
    private void VisitShowroom()
    {
        Console.WriteLine("1. The customer visits a
            dealer showroom.");
    }
    // The following method(step) will NOT vary
    private void GenerateBill()
    {
        Console.WriteLine("3. The bill is printed.");
    }
    private void DeliverProduct()
    {
        Console.WriteLine("4. The product is delivered.\n");
    }
    /*
    The following method will vary. It will be
    overridden by derived classes.
    */
    protected abstract void SelectProduct();

    // The template method
    public void PurchaseProduct()
    {
        // Step-1
        VisitShowroom();
        // Step-2: Specialized action
        SelectProduct();
        // Step-2.1: Eligible for gift?
```

```
        If (IsEligibleForGiftCoupon())
        {
            GenerateGiftCoupon();
        }
        // Step-3
        GenerateBill();
        // Step-4
        DeliverProduct();
    }

    protected void GenerateGiftCoupon()
    {
        Console.WriteLine("\tA gift coupon is generated.");
    }

    // Hook:
    // By default, there is no gift coupon.

    protected virtual bool IsEligibleForGiftCoupon()
    {
        return false;
    }
}

// The concrete derived class:Television
public class Television : Device
{

    // If a customer purchases a television
    // he/she can get a gift.
    protected override bool IsEligibleForGiftCoupon()
    {
        return true;
    }
```

```
    protected override void SelectProduct()
    {
        Console.WriteLine("2. The customer purchases a
            television.");
    }
}

// The concrete derived class:WashingMachine
public class WashingMachine : Device
{
    protected override void SelectProduct()
    {
        Console.WriteLine("2. The customer purchases a
            washing machine.");
    }
}
```

Output

Here is the output. Notice the effect of the hook method in bold:

```
***A demonstration of a template Method.***
```

```
---The customer wants a television.---
1. The customer visits a dealer showroom.
2. The customer purchases a television.
```
        A gift coupon is generated.
```
3. The bill is printed.
4. The product is delivered.
```

```
---The customer wants a washing machine.---
1. The customer visits a dealer showroom.
2. The customer purchases a washing machine.
3. The bill is printed.
4. The product is delivered.
```

Summary

This chapter showed you how to use a template method to make an efficient application. Then it shows how to use hooks to adapt to a new requirement without altering the core structure of an algorithm.

Hooks can make your program efficient, and they are common in sophisticated programs. For example, they can be used to process or modify system events. They can be useful to insert, remove, process, or modify keyboard and mouse events too.

Microsoft (see `https://docs.microsoft.com/en-us/archive/msdn-magazine/2002/october/cutting-edge-windows-hooks-in-the-net-framework`) says the following:

> *In Win32, a hook is a mechanism by which a user-defined function can intercept a handful of system events before they reach an application. Typical events that hooks can intercept include messages, mouse and keyboard actions, and opening and closing of windows. The hook can act on events and modify the actual flow of code.*

There is a downside too. If you are not careful, using hooks can impact the overall performance of your application. But in our case, using a hook method was beneficial. It helped us to extend the application to accommodate a new requirement.

CHAPTER 9

Simplify Complex Systems Using Facades

In Chapter 8, you saw how you can redefine some steps in a multistep algorithm to achieve a task. In this chapter, you will look at an application that also does a series of tasks. But instead of redefining these tasks, you will learn how to make a simplified interface to perform this task. Facades are useful in this context.

Note   You may be interested to understand the difference between a facade and a template method. In general, a template method belongs to a base class and allows the subclasses to redefine some steps. You create an object of a class and invoke this template method to complete your job. But facades often involve multiple objects from many different classes. This time you perform a series of steps to accomplish the task involving all these objects. You do not redefine the methods in these classes; instead, you manage to call them easily. So, a subsystem class often does not know about the presence of a facade.

Facades provide you with an entry point to access various methods across different classes in a structured manner. If you enforce a rule that does not allow you access to the individual methods directly and instead you access them through your facade only, then the facade is called an **opaque** facade; otherwise, it is a **transparent** facade. You can make your facade **static** too.

Author's Note   Depending on a programming language, you can make a top-level static class. For example, at the time of this writing, I was using the Java SE 17 edition. Up until this edition, you cannot tag the keyword `static` with a top-level class in Java. *Java Language Specification (Java SE 17 Edition) says*

© Vaskaran Sarcar 2023
V. Sarcar, *Simple and Efficient Programming with C#*, https://doi.org/10.1007/978-1-4842-8737-8_9

that the modifier static pertains only to member classes and local classes. Though
C# allows this, there are restrictions. For example, you cannot instantiate the
static class. Also, a static class can contain static members only, and there are
no instance constructors. Finally, it is sealed by nature. So, depending on the
programming language, you can make a top-level static class with static methods
to avoid direct instantiation of a facade class. And when you use a similar concept,
you say that you are using a static facade.

The Problem Statement

A person can apply for a loan from a bank. The bank must do some background
verification before it grants the loan to a customer. This background verification is a
complex process that consists of various subprocesses. If needed, the bank officials
can visit the customer's property too before they consider the loan application. If an
applicant fulfills all these criteria, they can get a loan. But here is the key: an applicant
does not know the details of the background verification and is interested in the final
outcome only, whether the loan is approved. How the bank officials reach the decision
does not matter to the customer. In the upcoming examples, you will see such a process.
For simplicity, I make the following assumptions:

- A loan applicant or customer must have some assets. If the asset
value is less than the loan application claimed, the customer cannot
get the loan.

- If a customer has an existing loan, the customer cannot get any
new loan.

Our job is to make an application that is based on these assumptions. Here is some
sample output for better clarity.

Case 1:

```
Bob's current asset value: $5,000.
He claims a loan amount: $20,000.
He has an existing loan.
```

Expected Outcome: Bob cannot get the loan for the following reasons:

- Insufficient balance.

- An old loan exists.

Case 2:

```
Jack's current asset value: $100,000.
He claims a loan amount: $30,000.
He has no existing loan.
```

Expected Outcome: Jack can get the loan.

Case 3:

```
Tony's current asset value: $125,000.
He claims a loan amount: $50,000.
He has an existing loan.
```

Expected Outcome: Tony cannot get the loan for the following reason:

- An old loan exists.

Let's build the application.

Initial Program

In this example, you see three classes: `Person`, `Asset`, and `LoanStatus`. An instance of the `Person` class can apply for a loan. This class has a constructor that takes three different parameters called `name`, `assetValue`, and `previousLoanExist`. To avoid more typing and passing all these three parameters during the instance creation, I made the last two parameters optional. Here is the `Person` class:

```
class Person
    {
        public string name;
        public double assetValue;
        public bool previousLoanExist;

        public Person(string name,
            double assetValue=100000,
```

```
            bool previousLoanExist = false)
    {
        this.name = name;
        this.assetValue = assetValue;
        this.previousLoanExist = previousLoanExist;
    }
}
```

Notice the constructor of this class. Since you have two optional parameters, you can create instances using any of the following lines:

```
Person jack = new Person("Jack");
Person kate = new Person("Kate", 70000);
Person tony = new Person("Tony", 125000,true);
```

See the Asset class now. This class has a method HasSufficientAssetValue to verify whether the current asset value is greater than or equal to the claim amount. Here is the Asset class:

```
class Asset
{
    public bool HasSufficientAssetValue(
                        Person person,
                        double claimAmount)
    {
        Console.WriteLine($"Validating {person.name}'s
          asset value.");
        return person.assetValue >= claimAmount;
    }
}
```

Now see the LoanStatus class. This class has a method called HasPreviousLoans to verify whether a person has an existing loan.

```
class LoanStatus
{
    public bool HasPreviousLoans(Person person)
    {
```

```
    Console.WriteLine($"Verifying {person.name}'s
     existing loan(s).");
    return !person.previousLoanExist;
  }
}
```

POINT TO NOTE

Notice that inside the `HasPreviousLoans` method of the `LoanStatus` class, I have used a simplified statement when I use the following:

```
return !person.previousLoanExist;
instead of using the following line:
return !person.previousLoanExist ? true : false;
```

I did the same inside the `HasSufficientAssetValue` method that belongs to the `Asset` class. Some readers are often confused when they see the "simplified" code. This is why I wanted to mention this.

Demonstration 1

The `Person`, `Asset`, and `LoanStatus` classes were already shown. So, I will not repeat these classes in the following code segment.

Note   For simplicity, I put all those three classes and the following client code into a single file. When you download the source code from the Apress website, refer to the folder `Demo1_WithoutFacade` inside `Chapter9` to see the complete program.

Now assume that a novice programmer writes the following client code. The programmer creates a `Person` instance, called `bob`, and shows whether he is eligible for a loan. It works, but is it a good solution? We'll analyze this.

```
Console.WriteLine("Directly interacting with the
 classes(subsystems).");
```

```csharp
Asset asset = new();
LoanStatus loanStatus = new();
string status = "approved";
string reason = string.Empty;
bool assetValue, previousLoanExist;

// Person-1
Person bob = new("Bob", 5000, true);

// Starts background verification
assetValue = asset.HasSufficientAssetValue(bob,20000);
previousLoanExist = loanStatus.HasPreviousLoans(bob);

if (!assetValue)
{
    status = "Not approved.";
    reason += "\nInsufficient balance.";
}
if (!previousLoanExist)
{
    status = "Not approved.";
    reason += "\nan old loan exists.";
}
Console.WriteLine($"{bob.name}'s application status: {status}");
Console.WriteLine($"Remarks if any: {reason}");
```

Output

Here is the output:

```
Directly interacting with the classes(subsystems).
Validating Bob's asset value.
Verifying Bob's existing loan(s).
Bob's application status: Not approved.
Remarks if any:
Insufficient balance.
An old loan exists.
```

Analysis

Let me ask you a few questions about this program.

- There is only one customer at this moment. What will the developer do if you have two or more loan applicants? Will the developer repeat the background verification logic multiple times inside the client code?

- Have you noticed that inside the client code the developer exposes the background verification logic? Is this a good idea?

- How would you feel if you do not need to create any subsystem instances (for example an `Asset` or `LoanStatus` instance) to know the outcome? Instead, assume that there is a loan approver instance that is the only point of contact to know the status of an application. It enables you to write something like the following:

```
Person bob = new("Bob", 5000, true);
string approvalStatus = loanApprover.
   CheckLoanEligibility(bob, 20000);
Console.WriteLine($"{bob.name}'s application
   status: {approvalStatus}");
```

- In the future, if there are new criteria to get a loan, the loan approver can take the responsibility to handle the situation. Will you value this point?

Better Program

When you analyze the questions, you'll search for a better solution. The last two questions give you the idea that making a single point of contact (like the loan approver I discussed) can make the code cleaner and easily maintainable. Let's see such an implementation in the upcoming demonstration. The `LoanApprover` class plays the role of the facade layer in this example. You'll see that the client code talks to this facade to know the final decision.

Class Diagram

Figure 9-1 shows the class diagram for demonstration 2.

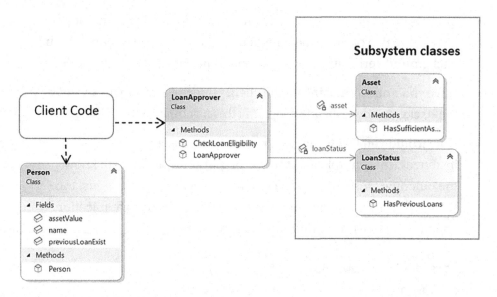

Figure 9-1. *The client code talks to the LoanApprover to know whether an applicant can get a new loan*

Demonstration 2

Here is the complete program:

```
Console.WriteLine("***Simplifying the usage of a
 complex system using a facade.***");
// Using a facade
LoanApprover loanApprover = new();

// Person-1
Person bob = new("Bob", 5000, true);
string approvalStatus = loanApprover.CheckLoanEligibility(bob, 20000);
Console.WriteLine($"{bob.name}'s application status: {approvalStatus}");

// Person-2
Person jack = new("Jack");
```

```
approvalStatus = loanApprover.CheckLoanEligibility(jack, 30000);
Console.WriteLine($"{jack.name}'s application status: {approvalStatus}");

// Person-3
Person tony = new("Tony", 125000, true);
approvalStatus = loanApprover.CheckLoanEligibility(tony, 50000);
Console.WriteLine($"{tony.name}'s application status: {approvalStatus}");

class Person
{
    public string name;
    public double assetValue;
    public bool previousLoanExist;

    public Person(string name,
        double assetValue = 100000,
        bool previousLoanExist = false)
    {
        this.name = name;
        this.assetValue = assetValue;
        this.previousLoanExist = previousLoanExist;
    }
}

class Asset
{
    public bool HasSufficientAssetValue(Person person,
     double claimAmount)
    {
        Console.WriteLine($"Validating {person.name}'s
          asset value.");
        return person.assetValue >= claimAmount;
    }
}

class LoanStatus
{
    public bool HasPreviousLoans(Person person)
```

```csharp
    {
        Console.WriteLine($"Verifying {person.name}'s
          existing loan(s).");
        return !person.previousLoanExist;
    }
}

class LoanApprover
{
    readonly Asset asset;
    readonly LoanStatus loanStatus;
    public LoanApprover()
    {
        asset = new Asset();
        loanStatus = new LoanStatus();
    }
    public string CheckLoanEligibility(Person person,
     double claimAmount)
    {
        string status = "Approved";
        string reason = String.Empty;
        Console.WriteLine($"\nChecking loan
         approval status of {person.name}.");
        // Using raw string literals in C# 11 (Preview)
        Console.WriteLine($"""
         [Current Status of the applicant:
          Asset value:${person.assetValue}.
          Claim amount:${claimAmount}.
          Has existing loan(s)?:
                    {person.previousLoanExist}.
         ]
         """);

        if (!asset.HasSufficientAssetValue(person,
         claimAmount))
```

```
        {
            status = "Not approved.";
            reason += "\nInsufficient balance.";
        }
        if (!loanStatus.HasPreviousLoans(person))
        {
            status = "Not approved.";
            reason += "\nOld loan exists.";
        }

        return string.Concat(status, "\nRemarks if
          any:", reason);
    }
}
```

Output

Here is the output:

```
***Simplifying the usage of a complex system using a
 facade.***

Checking loan approval status of Bob.
[Current Status of the applicant:
 Asset value:$5000.
 Claim amount:$20000.
 Has existing loan(s)?:True.
]
Validating Bob's asset value.
Verifying Bob's existing loan(s).
Bob's application status: Not approved.
Remarks if any:
Insufficient balance.
An old loan exists.

Checking loan approval status of Jack.
[Current Status of the applicant:
```

```
 Asset value:$100000.
 Claim amount:$30000.
 Has existing loan(s)?:False.
]
Validating Jack's asset value.
Verifying Jack's existing loan(s).
Jack's application status: Approved
Remarks if any:

Checking loan approval status of Tony.
[Current Status of the applicant:
 Asset value:$125000.
 Claim amount:$50000.
 Has existing loan(s)?:True.
]
Validating Tony's asset value.
Verifying Tony's existing loan(s).
Tony's application status: Not approved.
Remarks if any:
An old loan exists.
```

Analysis

Using facades, you get the following benefits:

- You can create a simplified interface for your clients.

- You reduce the number of objects that a client needs to deal with.

- If there are a large number of subsystems, managing those subsystems with a facade can make communication easier.

Summary

This chapter shows you how to use a facade in an application. You learned that a facade can help you develop a simplified interface for your clients when you need to deal with many subsystems. I also discussed the difference between a facade and a template method. It's worth remembering the following points before you consider using a facade in an application:

- You should not assume that you can have only one facade in an application. You can use two or more of them if you find them useful.

- One facade can show a different behavior from another facade. For example, you may allow or disallow direct access to subsystems. When you force the client to create instances through a facade, it is called an **opaque** facade. When you also allow direct access to the subsystems, it is called a **transparent** facade.

- But what happens if you allow a client to talk to the subsystem classes directly? You make your code "dirty" and often expose the program logic.

- On the contrary, when you restrict this direct communication, you add the costs for maintaining a separate layer. If a subsystem changes, you need to incorporate the corresponding behavior in the facade layer.

- In addition, you need to test this layer before you deliver the product to a customer. If the facade is too complex, it can produce some additional maintenance costs.

PART IV

Handling Surprises in a Better Way

Handling errors is an unavoidable part of programming. Particularly, runtime exceptions are dangerous, and often they appear in the form of `NullReferenceException` in C#.

Part IV focuses on these topics and provides useful suggestions about how to handle them in a better way. It consists of two chapters, in which we'll try to find out the answers to some important questions, such as the following:

- How can we organize exceptions to handle different exceptions in the same way?

- How can we organize exceptions to handle the same exception in a different way?

- Why do we need these arrangements?

- How can you handle null values and avoid repetitive null checks effectively?

Understanding and analyzing them with different case studies will make you a better programmer.

CHAPTER 10

Organizing Exceptions

Errors in a program can be classified into the following categories: compile-time errors and runtime errors. Compile-time errors are comparatively easy to fix because you know about them much earlier (i.e., at compile time). These may occur mainly due to syntax errors or typing mistakes. The compiler can point to them so that you can take corrective measures immediately. By contrast, runtime errors are dangerous because you encounter them when a program is executing. Programmatically, we call them *exceptions*. Since the program was compiled earlier, you expected it to run successfully. Why do exceptions occur? These may occur through some careless mistakes; maybe you have implemented the wrong logic, you have ignored some loopholes in the code paths of the program, etc. This type of error is tough to handle and is costly. Even after our best efforts, often these situations are unavoidable. It is also true that many of the failures are beyond the control of a programmer. So, handling these runtime errors is essential when you write an application. C#'s exception handling mechanism is important because it helps you deal with these typical runtime errors in advance.

POINTS TO NOTE

In C#, when you encounter a runtime error, the code that discovered the problem will package up the necessary information about the problem into a special object. This is the "exception" object that is either an instance of the Exception class or a class derived from the Exception class. Any of the following can cause these exceptional situations: the common language runtime (CLR), .NET, a third-party library, or application code.

© Vaskaran Sarcar 2023
V. Sarcar, *Simple and Efficient Programming with C#*, https://doi.org/10.1007/978-1-4842-8737-8_10

The focus of this chapter is not to discuss the basics of exception handling in C#. I assume that you know how we deal with them. Instead, after a quick review, we'll discuss a few code segments that work properly, but as a developer, you can improve them. Broadly, I'll discuss the following situations:

- **Case 1:** You catch different exceptions but want to handle them in the same way.

- **Case 2:** You catch the same exception, but you want to handle it differently based on the situation.

Recap of Exceptions

Before we discuss these cases, let me remind you about the following points. These are important to avoid any confusion before you read further.

- You use the following keywords to deal with C# exceptions: `try`, `catch`, `throw`, and `finally`. In addition, starting with C# 6.0, you can use the contextual keyword `when` in a `catch` statement to filter an exception.

- You can guard an exception using a `try-catch` block. The code that may throw an exception is placed inside a `try` block, and this exceptional situation is handled inside a `catch` block.

- The code in the `finally` block must execute (unless you write some awkward code). In general, this block is placed after a `try` block or a `try-catch` block.

- When an exception is raised inside a `try` block, the control jumps to the respective `catch` or `finally` block. The remaining part of the `try` block will not be executed.

- You can associate multiple `catch` blocks with a `try` block. In this case, you must place them from the most specific to the least specific types.

Enough review! Let's start analyzing the case studies.

Case 1: Handling Different Exceptions in the Same Way

Let's assume you have a third-party code. You want to use a dynamic link library (DLL) in your program. To make things simple, I have written the following code, which we intend to reuse in the upcoming program:

```
using System.Runtime.Serialization;

namespace RemoteNumberProcessor
{
    public class RemoteProcessor
    {
        private int _number;
        public RemoteProcessor(int number)
        {
            _number = number;
            // Some other code, if any
        }
        public void ProcessNumber()
        {
            if (_number < 0)
                throw new NumberTooSmallException
                ($"The input {_number} is less than
                 the lower boundary(00.");
            else if (_number > 100)
                throw new NumberTooBigException
                ($"The input {_number} is greater
                 than the upper boundary (100).");
            else if (50 < _number && _number < 60)
                throw new ReservedNumberException
                ($"The input is {_number}.The numbers
                 51 to 59 are reserved for
                 special uses.");
            else
                Console.WriteLine($"The input
```

```csharp
            {_number} is valid. Processing it.");
    }
}

[Serializable]
public class ReservedNumberException : Exception
{
    public ReservedNumberException(string?
     message) : base(message)
    {
    }
    // Other overloaded versions of
    // ReservedNumberException are not shown here
}

[Serializable]
public class NumberTooBigException : Exception
{
    public NumberTooBigException(string? message)
     : base(message)
    {
    }

    // Other overloaded versions of
    // NumberTooBigException are not shown here
}

[Serializable]
public class NumberTooSmallException : Exception
{
    public NumberTooSmallException(string?
     message) : base(message)
    {
    }

    // Other overloaded versions of
    // NumberTooSmallException are not shown here
}
}
```

> **Note**   I haven't shown you all the overloaded versions of constructors in the previous code segment. I generated them automatically in Visual Studio to speed up my coding, but I have not used all of them. But when you download the source code from the Apress website, you can see them all. The same comment applies to similar code segments in this chapter.

Initial Program

Let's consider the following program that uses the previous code. When you download the Demo1 project of Chapter 10 from the Apress website, you'll see that I added the RemoteNumberProcessor project reference to this file. See Figure 10-1.

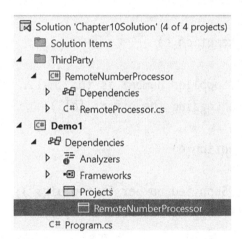

Figure 10-1.   *The project reference RemoteNumberProcessor is added to Demo1*

Now go through the complete program. Check whether you can improve this program.

Demonstration 1

Here is the complete demonstration:

```
using RemoteNumberProcessor;

Console.WriteLine("Chapter 10.Demo-1.");
// Testing the input values:39,-2,57,150
// RemoteProcessor processor = new(39);
// RemoteProcessor processor = new(-2);
RemoteProcessor processor = new(57);
// RemoteProcessor processor = new(150);
try
{
    processor.ProcessNumber();
}
catch (NumberTooSmallException e)
{
    Console.WriteLine("Supplied number is too small.");
    Console.WriteLine($"Logging the error: {e}");
}
catch (NumberTooBigException e)
{
    Console.WriteLine("Supplied number is too big.");
    Console.WriteLine($"Logging the error: {e}");
}
catch (ReservedNumberException e)
{
    Console.WriteLine("Tried to use a special number.");
    Console.WriteLine($"Logging the error: {e}");
}
finally
{
    // Some clean-up code
}
```

Output

Here is the output when you test the value 57 (I have commented out other lines that test the values 39, -2, and 150). I placed and executed all these programs in my E:\ drive, so you see this location in this output.

```
Chapter 10.Demo-1.
Tried to use a special number.
Logging the error: RemoteNumberProcessor.
ReservedNumberException: The input is 57. The numbers
51 to 59 are reserved for special uses.
 at RemoteNumberProcessor.RemoteProcessor.
 ProcessNumber() in
 E:\MyPrograms\SimpleCSharp2E\Chapter10\Chapter10Solution\
   RemoteNumberProcessor\RemoteProcessor.cs:line 20 at
   Program.<Main>$(String[] args) in
 E:\MyPrograms\SimpleCSharp2E\Chapter10\Chapter10Solution\
   Demo1\Program.cs:line 11
```

Analysis

Have you noticed the catch blocks? Yes, there are different messages, but what do they do? They try to show and log the error (I have shown only console statements instead of calling an actual logger function to keep this simple). So, all these catch blocks try to do similar activities. As a result, you can see lots of repetition. How can we make this code better? Let's see the next program.

Better Program

One of my favorite books is *Clean Code*. There is a chapter on error handling written by Michael Feathers. In that chapter, the author uses a wrapper to remove the redundancy from a code segment. He also writes the following:

> *In fact, wrapping third-party APIs is a best practice.*

Here we try to implement the same idea using C# code. In Chapter 7 of this book, you learned about wrappers. So, you should not be surprised when you see the following code:

```
public class LocalProcessor
  {
      private RemoteProcessor processor;
      public LocalProcessor(int number)
      {
          processor = new RemoteProcessor(number);
      }
      public void ProcessNumber()
      {
          try
          {
              processor.ProcessNumber();
          }
          catch (NumberTooSmallException e)
          {
              throw new InvalidInputException(e.Message);
          }
          catch (NumberTooBigException e)
          {
              throw new InvalidInputException(e.Message);
          }
          catch (ReservedNumberException e)
          {
              throw new InvalidInputException(e.Message);
          }

          finally
          {
              // Some clean-up code
          }
      }
  }
```

What is the benefit when the `LocalProcessor` wraps the `RemoteProcessor` in the previous code? The answer is that this time you can write the following code:

```
try
{
    processor.ProcessNumber();
}
catch (InvalidInputException e)
{
    Console.WriteLine("Invalid number.");
    Console.WriteLine($"Logging the error:{e}");
}
finally
{
    // Some clean-up code
}
```

Can you see the benefits? If not, read the following points:

- The code is simple and easy to understand.

- You can return a common exception type; so, you are handling it in one way. There is no redundancy.

- You minimize your dependency on third-party code. You can opt for a different vendor without much penalty. Notice that the previous code segment is closed for modification.

Demonstration 2

Here is demonstration 2. It is a modified version of demonstration 1. Like the previous cases, you can download the complete code from the Apress website. The code for this project is placed inside the folder `Chapter10`. See Figure 10-2.

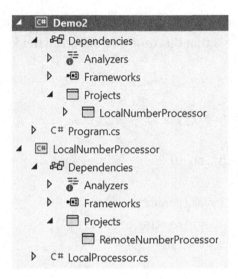

Figure 10-2. *The Solution Explorer view for the Demo2 project*

I show you both the files here for your easy reference.

// Program.cs(in Demo2)

```
using LocalNumberProcessor;

Console.WriteLine("Chapter 10.Demo-2.");
//LocalProcessor processor = new(39);
//LocalProcessor processor = new(-2);
//LocalProcessor processor = new(57);
LocalProcessor processor = new(150);

try
{
    processor.ProcessNumber();
}
catch (InvalidInputException e)
{
    Console.WriteLine("Invalid number.");
    Console.WriteLine($"Logging the error: {e}");
}
```

```
finally
{
    // Some clean-up code
}
```

// LocalNumberProcessor.cs

```
using RemoteNumberProcessor;
using System.Runtime.Serialization;

namespace LocalNumberProcessor
{
    public class LocalProcessor
    {
        private RemoteProcessor processor;
        public LocalProcessor(int number)
        {
            processor = new RemoteProcessor(number);
        }
        public void ProcessNumber()
        {
            try
            {
                processor.ProcessNumber();
            }
            catch (NumberTooSmallException e)
            {
                throw new InvalidInputException(e.Message);
            }
            catch (NumberTooBigException e)
            {
                throw new InvalidInputException(e.Message);
            }
            catch (ReservedNumberException e)
            {
```

```csharp
                throw new InvalidInputException(e.Message);
            }
            finally
            {
                // Some clean-up code
            }
        }
    }

    [Serializable]
    public class InvalidInputException : Exception
    {
        public InvalidInputException()
        {
        }

        public InvalidInputException(string? Message)
         : base(message)
        {
        }

        // Other overloaded versions of
        // InvalidInputException are not shown here
}
```

Output

Here is the output when you test the value 57 (I have commented out other lines that test the values 39, -2, and 150):

```
Chapter 10.Demo-2.
Invalid number.
Logging the error: LocalNumberProcessor.
  InvalidInputException: The input is 57.The numbers
  51 to 59 are reserved for special uses.
   at LocalNumberProcessor.LocalProcessor.ProcessNumber()
 in E:\MyPrograms\SimpleCSharp2E\Chapter10\
```

```
Chapter10Solution\LocalNumberProcessor\
LocalProcessor.cs:line 29
  at
Program.<Main>$(String[] args) in E:\MyPrograms\SimpleCSharp2E\Chapter10\
Chapter10Solution\Demo2\Program.cs:line 11
```

Analysis

From the output of demonstration 2, you can see that you have received sufficient information about the exception. This modified demonstration is easy to read and understand. In addition, you have removed the duplicate code/logic that was visible in demonstration 1.

Case 2: Handling the Same Exception in Different Ways

This time we'll discuss the opposite case: you'll see the same exception that is handled in different ways. Before that, let me remind you that I'll try to mimic these situations with some dummy code and console messages. My focus is to discuss the scenarios with short and easy examples. Let's start.

Initial Program

The following program throws a user-defined exception, called `CustomWebException`. To mimic some typical situations, I use a random number generator before I throw this exception. Here I consider only two cases such as a temporary error and a protocol error.

Demonstration 3

Here is the complete demonstration:

```
using System.Runtime.Serialization;

Console.WriteLine("Chapter 10.Demo-3.");

Console.WriteLine("***A case study on exception filters.***");
```

```
try
{
    int a = 10;
    // Returns a random number between 0(inclusive)
    // and 2(exclusive)

    int b = new Random().Next(0, 2);
    Console.WriteLine($"b={b}");

    int c = b > 0 ?
     throw new CustomWebException("Protocol error") :
     throw new CustomWebException("Temporary error");
    Console.WriteLine("Thank you.");
}
catch (Exception ex)
{
    Console.WriteLine($"Caught: {ex.GetType()}");
    Console.WriteLine($"Exception message:{ex.Message}");
}
finally
{
    // Some clean-up code
}

[Serializable]
public class CustomWebException : Exception
{
    public CustomWebException()
    {
    }

    public CustomWebException(string? message)
        : base(message)
    {
    }
```

```
    // Other overloaded versions of
    // CustomWebException are not shown here
}
```

Output

Here is a sample output (used to show the temporary error):

```
Chapter 10.Demo-3.
***A case study on exception filters.***
b=0
Caught: CustomWebException
Exception message: Temporary error
```

Here is another output (used to show the protocol error):

```
Chapter 10.Demo-3.
***A case study on exception filters.***
b=1
Caught: CustomWebException
Exception message: Protocol error
```

Analysis

Since the exception is the same, we handled it in the same catch block. But did you notice that we throw the same exception for different reasons? Can we handle them differently?

You may think, why do we need to do this? Consider a situation when you do not worry about a temporary error. You believe that when a server is down, it may happen. So, **what do you do if apart from just logging this case, you do not want to write any specific code to handle this particular situation? In other words, you allow this exception to occur because you do not worry about it.** Let's see the next program.

Better Program

This time you can use exception filters. They are supported starting with C# 6.0.

Demonstration 4

To fulfill this specific requirement (which is mentioned earlier), here I present a new program for you. This time you'll see a static method Log(..) that logs the specific error and returns false. As a result, the corresponding catch block will not be executed. Similar to previous programs, you can download the complete code from the Apress website. This code is placed inside the folder Chapter10.

```
using System.Net;

Console.WriteLine("Chapter 10.Demo-4.");

Console.WriteLine("***A case study on exception filters.***");
try
{
    int a = 10;
    // Returns a random number between 0(inclusive)
    // and 2(exclusive)
    int b = new Random().Next(0, 2);
    Console.WriteLine($"b={b}");
    int c = b > 0 ?
     throw new CustomWebException("Protocol error") :
     throw new CustomWebException("Temporary error");
    Console.WriteLine("Thank you.");
}

catch (Exception ex) when (ex.Message.Contains("Protocol"))
{
    Console.WriteLine($"Caught: {ex.GetType()}");
    Console.WriteLine($"Exception message:{ex.Message}");
}

catch (Exception ex) when (Logger.Log(ex))
{
}
finally
{
```

```
    // Some clean-up code
}

class Logger
{
    public static bool Log(Exception ex)
    {
        Console.WriteLine($"Logging the following
          exception.:");
        Console.WriteLine($"Caught: {ex.GetType()}");
        Console.WriteLine($"Exception message:{ex.Message}");
        return false;
    }
}

[Serializable]
public class CustomWebException : Exception
{
    public CustomWebException()
    {
    }

    public CustomWebException(string? message)
      : base(message)
    {
    }

    // Other overloaded versions of
    // CustomWebException are not shown here
}
```

Output

Here is some sample output:

```
Chapter 10.Demo-4.
***A case study on exception filters.***
```

```
b=1
Caught: CustomWebException
Exception message:Protocol error
```

But when b=0, you'll notice the window in Figure 10-3 that shows you the unhandled exception.

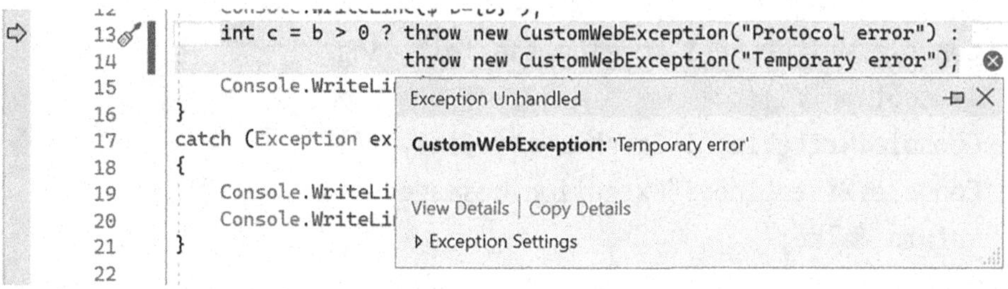

Figure 10-3. A runtime exception occurred in the program

Analysis

You can see that the output of demonstration 4 does not show any change when there is a protocol error (b=1), but the exception is unhandled when there is a temporary error (b=0). Though you did not handle the exception, you logged it properly. In short, you caught the same exception but processed it differently based on your needs.

Summary

Exception handling is an integral part of programming, and you cannot avoid it. This chapter did not discuss the basics of exception handling in C#. Instead, we focused on handling exceptions in a cleaner way and considered the following cases:

- **Case 1:** You caught different exceptions but handled them in the same way.

- **Case 2:** You caught the same exception but handled it differently based on the situation.

These case studies will help you write a better code for your application.

Special Attention to the Null Values

In the previous chapter, I told you about runtime exceptions. These are dangerous. Most often, they come in the form of the `NullReferenceException` in C#. Similarly, Java has the `NullPointerException`. The exception names can be different, but at the core, they arise when you try to access a member of an object whose value is `null`. Michael Feathers wrote the following in the book *Clean Code*:

> *Returning `null` from methods is bad, but passing `null` into methods is worse. Unless you are working with an API which expects you to pass `null`, you should avoid passing `null` in your code whenever possible.*

In short, these `null` values can kill an application prematurely. So, you need to handle them properly. This chapter focuses on them and provides you with some useful suggestions.

Initial Program

Suppose that `IVehicle` is an interface that has a method called `ShowStatus()`. Two concrete classes, `Bus` and `Train`, inherit from this interface and provide the implementation for this interface method. Here is the code segment that reflects this:

```
interface IVehicle
{
    void ShowStatus();
}
class Bus : IVehicle
{
    public void ShowStatus()
```

© Vaskaran Sarcar 2023
V. Sarcar, *Simple and Efficient Programming with C#*, https://doi.org/10.1007/978-1-4842-8737-8_11

```
    {
        Console.WriteLine("One bus is ready to travel.");
    }
}
class Train : IVehicle
{
    public void ShowStatus()
    {
        Console.WriteLine("One train is ready to travel.");
    }
}
```

For simplicity, I want clients of this program to create three IVehicle instances and invoke the corresponding ShowStatus method. Let's assume clients of this program can type b and t (in a console application) to create a Bus object and a Train object, respectively. Can you write this program? I know that you can. But before you write your program, let's investigate the following program. This program has a potential bug, and we'll improve it for sure, but you can see the importance of using null checks to avoid runtime errors in a program.

Demonstration 1

Here is the complete demonstration:

```
Console.WriteLine("Chapter 11.Demo-1.");
Console.WriteLine("This program has a potential bug.");
IVehicle[] vehicles = new IVehicle[3];
int vehicleCount = 0;
while (vehicleCount < 3)
{
    Console.WriteLine("Enter your choice(Type 'b' for
     a bus, 't' for a train.");
    string input = Console.ReadLine();
    switch (input)
    {
```

```csharp
        case "b":
            vehicles[vehicleCount] = new Bus();
            break;
        case "t":
            vehicles[vehicleCount] = new Train();
            break;
        default:
            Console.WriteLine("Invalid input");
            break;
    }
    vehicleCount++;
}

Console.WriteLine("**Checking the vehicle's status sequentially:**");
foreach (IVehicle vehicle in vehicles)
{
    vehicle.ShowStatus();
}

interface IVehicle
{
    void ShowStatus();
}
class Bus : IVehicle
{
    public void ShowStatus()
    {
        Console.WriteLine("One bus is ready to travel.");
    }
}
class Train : IVehicle
{
    public void ShowStatus()
    {
```

```
        Console.WriteLine("One train is ready to travel.");
    }
}
```

Output

This program does not show any errors if you pass valid inputs. Here is a sample:

```
Chapter 11.Demo-1.
This program has a potential bug.
Enter your choice(Type 'b' for a bus, 't' for a train.)
b
Enter your choice(Type 'b' for a bus, 't' for a train.)
t
Enter your choice(Type 'b' for a bus, 't' for a train.)
t
**Checking the vehicle's status sequentially:**
One bus is ready to travel.
One train is ready to travel.
One train is ready to travel.
```

Let's assume that, by mistake, the user has supplied a different character, say *e*, as shown here:

```
Chapter 11.Demo-1.
This program has a potential bug.
Enter your choice(Type 'b' for a bus, 't' for a train.)
b
Enter your choice(Type 'b' for a bus, 't' for a train.)
t
Enter your choice(Type 'b' for a bus, 't' for a train.)
e
```

This time you will see the following runtime exception:

System.NullReferenceException: 'Object reference not set to an instance of an object'.

Analysis

To avoid the previous runtime error, an immediate fix may come into your mind, as shown here:

```
if (vehicle != null)
{
  vehicle.ShowStatus();
}
```

This solution will work in this case. But think of an enterprise application. When you do null checks for each possible scenario, if you place if conditions like this, you make your code "dirty." At the same time, you may notice the side effect of the code being difficult to maintain. Is there a better solution? I think, yes. You can use the **null conditional operator (for member access)** as follows:

```
vehicle?.ShowStatus();
```

This operator is available in C# 6 and later versions only. It provides you with a lot of help. **Still, using the previous code segment, you can avoid the** NullReferenceException, **but you may not see the status of all the vehicles.** To understand this better, consider the following output now:

```
Chapter 11.Demo-1.
This program has a potential bug.
Enter your choice(Type 'b' for a bus, 't' for a train.)
b
Enter your choice(Type 'b' for a bus, 't' for a train.)
t
Enter your choice(Type 'b' for a bus, 't' for a train.)
e
Invalid input
**Checking the vehicle's status sequentially:**
One bus is ready to travel.
One train is ready to travel.
```

So, there are situations where instead of doing nothing, you want to provide a default behavior that suits your application. For example, in this case, instead of showing nothing, you may like to show that the vehicle is not ready yet. This is helpful because as per the requirements, clients need to see the status of all vehicles, but if they cannot see one (or more) of them, they will be clueless about this. **In a situation like this, you'll want to know about the Null Object pattern, which is covered next.**

Better Programs

Using the Null Object pattern, you can implement a "do-nothing" relationship, or you can provide a default behavior when an application encounters a null object instead of a real object. The core aim is to make a better solution by avoiding a "null objects check." Figure 11-1 shows a basic structure of this pattern.

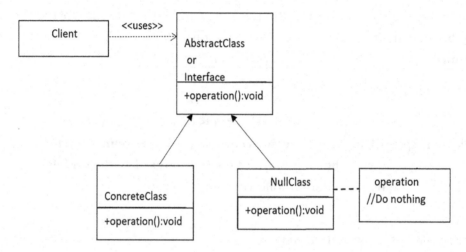

Figure 11-1. *The basic structure of the Null Object pattern*

Let's modify the faulty program that you saw in demonstration 1. This time you'll tackle an invalid input using a IncompleteVehicle object. Whenever the user supplies invalid data, the application will ignore it, and instead of creating a Bus or Train object, it'll use an IncompleteVehicle object. The class is defined as follows:

```
class IncompleteVehicle : IVehicle
{
    public void ShowStatus()
    {
        Console.WriteLine("This vehicle is incomplete.");
    }
}
```

POINTS TO REMEMBER

For any null object method, you need to return whatever seems sensible as a default. In our example, you cannot travel with an `IVehicle` object that is not created with valid input. So, it makes sense that the `ShowStatus()` method of the `IncompleteVehicle` class shows that it is not ready yet.

Let's take a look at the complete demonstration.

Demonstration 2

This is a modified version of demonstration 1. I have marked important changes in bold.

```
Console.WriteLine("Chapter 11.Demo-2.");
IVehicle[] vehicles = new IVehicle[3];
int vehicleCount = 0;
while (vehicleCount < 3)
{
    Console.WriteLine("Enter your choice(Type 'b' for
      a bus, 't' for a train.)");
    string input = Console.ReadLine();
    switch (input)
    {
        case "b":
            vehicles[vehicleCount] = new Bus();
            break;
        case "t":
            vehicles[vehicleCount] = new Train();
            break;
        default:
            Console.WriteLine("Invalid input");
            vehicles[vehicleCount] = new IncompleteVehicle();
            break;
    }
```

```csharp
        vehicleCount++;
}

Console.WriteLine("**Checking the vehicle's status sequentially:**");
foreach (IVehicle vehicle in vehicles)
{
    vehicle.ShowStatus();
}

interface IVehicle
{
    void ShowStatus();
}
class Bus : IVehicle
{
    public void ShowStatus()
    {
        Console.WriteLine("One bus is ready to travel.");
    }
}
class Train : IVehicle
{
    public void ShowStatus()
    {
        Console.WriteLine("One train is ready to travel.");
    }
}

class IncompleteVehicle : IVehicle
{
    public void ShowStatus()
    {
        Console.WriteLine("This vehicle cannot travel.");
    }
}
```

Output

This program does not show any error for valid input. Also, it does not halt whenever you pass an invalid input by mistake. Here is a sample:

```
Chapter 11.Demo-2.
Enter your choice(Type 'b' for a bus, 't' for a
 train.)
b
Enter your choice(Type 'b' for a bus, 't' for a
 train.)
gh
Invalid input
Enter your choice(Type 'b' for a bus, 't' for a
 train.)
t
**Checking the vehicle's status sequentially:**
One bus is ready to travel.
This vehicle cannot travel.
One train is ready to travel.
```

Analysis

The problem of demonstration 1 is gone! Also, you can see the status of all vehicles using the Null Object pattern too. **Truly, these were the key intentions of this chapter.**

Still, demonstration 2 can be improved. Why?

- In this application, for each invalid input, you create an IncompleteVehicle object. Now think about an enterprise application where users can pass many invalid inputs. In every case, if you create the same type of objects to tackle them, a large number of objects will be created unnecessarily, and they can affect the application performance.

So, what is the solution? Following the Singleton design pattern, you can create only one object, and from that time onward, you'll reuse it. The detailed discussion of the Singleton pattern is beyond the scope of this book, but I'll show you a modified version of the IncompleteVehicle class that you can use in this program to avoid unnecessary object creations. In the following demonstration, you'll see this class and its usage.

Demonstration 3

This is a modified version of demonstration 2. I have marked important changes in bold.

```
Console.WriteLine("Chapter 11.Demo-2(Modified version).");
IVehicle[] vehicles = new IVehicle[3];
int vehicleCount = 0;
while (vehicleCount < 3)
{
    Console.WriteLine("Enter your choice(Type 'b' for
     a bus, 't' for a train.)");
    string input = Console.ReadLine();
    switch (input)
    {
        case "b":
            vehicles[vehicleCount] = new Bus();
            break;
        case "t":
            vehicles[vehicleCount] = new Train();
            break;
        default:
            Console.WriteLine("Invalid input");
            vehicles[vehicleCount] = IncompleteVehicle.Instance;
            break;
    }
    vehicleCount++;
}
```

```csharp
Console.WriteLine("**Checking the vehicle's status sequentially:**");
foreach (IVehicle vehicle in vehicles)
{
    vehicle.ShowStatus();
}

interface IVehicle
{
    void ShowStatus();
}
class Bus : IVehicle
{
    public void ShowStatus()
    {
        Console.WriteLine("One bus is ready to travel.");
    }
}
class Train : IVehicle
{
    public void ShowStatus()
    {
        Console.WriteLine("One train is ready to travel.");
    }
}
class IncompleteVehicle : IVehicle
{
    private static readonly IncompleteVehicle instance = new();
    public static IncompleteVehicle Instance
    {
        get
        {
            return instance;
        }
    }
    public void ShowStatus()
    {
```

```
        Console.WriteLine("This vehicle cannot travel.");
    }
}
```

Analysis

This program produces the same output that you saw in demonstration 2. I have not repeated those lines here. The difference is that this program can create at most one IncompleteVehicle instance. If needed, it'll reuse this instance again.

POINTS TO NOTE

In this demonstration, I talked about the Null Object pattern. It is useful to remember that there is a pattern called the Special Case pattern. These two concepts are very close. Why? A special case is made when a subclass provides special behavior for a particular case. In fact, the book *Patterns of Enterprise Application Architecture* says the following:

I haven't seen Special Case written up as a pattern yet, but Null Object has been written up in [Woolf]. If you'll pardon the unresistable pun, I see Null Object as special case of Special Case.

To describe the intent of the Null Object pattern, Bobby Woolf writes the following (see https://www.cs.oberlin.edu/~jwalker/refs/woolf.ps):

Provide a surrogate for another object that shares the same interface but does nothing. The Null Object encapsulates the implementation decisions of how to "do nothing" and hides those details from its collaborators.

Now you may think that since I have implemented a special behavior instead of a "do-nothing" behavior, I could call it a Special Case pattern instead of a Null Object pattern. Probably you are correct. But the overall philosophy is the same because for me, doing nothing also depicts a special kind of behavior. This is why instead of memorizing a pattern name, let's focus on why we see different pattern names. The idea behind this is that there are situations where a null can mean different things. For example, consider the cases such as "incomplete data versus wrong data" or "a missing customer versus an invalid customer." Instead of treating everything as a null customer, you can use the concept of a special customer.

Summary

Runtime errors are dangerous, and often they come in the form of `NullReferenceException` in C#. So, handling the null values is an important aspect of programming. This chapter discussed them using some simple code fragments and provided a better solution.

In short, this chapter answered the following questions:

- How can a program raise `NullReferenceException` in C#?

- How can you avoid repeated null checks using a traditional `if-else` chain?

- How can you provide default behavior (or a do-nothing behavior) for the null values using the Null Object pattern?

- How can you avoid unnecessary object creations when you deal with the null values?

Before I finish writing this chapter, I want to mention the following points too:

- The Null Object pattern basically helps you to implement a default behavior when you unconsciously deal with an object that is not present at all. But trying to supply such a default behavior may not be appropriate always. There are situations when you like to fix the root cause of a failure. In that case, throwing a `NullReferenceException` can make more sense to you. In this case, you can handle the exception in a `try-catch` block or a `try-catch-finally` block and update the log information accordingly.

- Incorrect implementations of the Null Object pattern can suppress the true bug that may appear normal in program execution.

So, in the end, it heavily depends on your mindset about how to handle the null values in an application.

PART V

The Road Ahead

Part V consists of three chapters, in which we'll try to find out the answers to some important questions, such as the following:

- How does garbage collection work in C#?

- How can we identify and tackle memory leaks in an application?

- How can we decide between a static method and an instance method?

- Why is understanding design patterns important?

- How can we avoid anti-patterns?

In addition, we will go through some Q&A sessions and become familiar with some terms in the context of software development. A quick overview of these topics can help you to think better and program better in the future.

CHAPTER 12

Memory Management

Memory management is an important concern for a developer, and it is a very big topic. This chapter will touch on the important points in a simplified manner to help you understand memory management in programming.

Following some design guidelines while making an application is not enough; that is only one part of the equation. An application is truly efficient when there is no memory leak. If a computer program runs over a long time but fails to release memory resources that are no longer needed, you can see the impact of the memory leaks. Here are some common symptoms:

- A machine becomes slow over time.

- A specific operation in an application takes longer to execute.

- The worst case is that an application/system can crash.

But before we discuss memory leaks, it'll be helpful if you can clarify your understanding of memory allocations and deallocations. **A novice C# programmer often believes that the garbage collector (GC) can take care of memory management in every possible scenario. This is not true, and unfortunately, it is a common mistake.** This chapter will cover this and also help you understand the cause of memory leaks, which we'll discuss in Chapter 13.

Overview

In a programming language like C++, you deallocate the memory once the intended job is completed to avoid memory leaks. But .NET always tries to make your programming life easier. It has a garbage collector that clears the objects that do not have any use after a particular point. In programming, they are called **dirty objects** or **unreferenced objects**.

© Vaskaran Sarcar 2023
V. Sarcar, *Simple and Efficient Programming with C#*, https://doi.org/10.1007/978-1-4842-8737-8_12

How does the garbage collector clear the dirty objects? In C#, the heap memory is managed. This means the CLR takes care of this responsibility. In the managed code, CLR's garbage collector does this job for you, and you do not have to deallocate the managed memory. It removes the unused stuff on the heap and recollects the memory for further use. The garbage collector program runs in the background as a low-priority thread. It keeps track of the dirty objects for you. The .NET runtime on regular intervals can invoke this program to remove unreferenced or dirty objects from memory. At a given point in time, if an object has no reference, the garbage collector marks this object and reclaims the memory occupied by the object, assuming that it is no longer needed.

Note   In theory, when a local variable references an object, it's ready for garbage collection at the earliest point at which it is no longer needed. But if you disable the optimization in debug mode, the lifetime of the object extends to the end of the block. But garbage collection may not reclaim the memory immediately. There are various factors that affect this, such as available memory and the time since the last collection. This means an orphaned object can be released immediately, or there may be some delay that may vary.

However, there is a catch. Some objects require special code to release resources. Here are some common examples: you open a file, perform some reading or writing, but forget to close the file. A similar kind of attention is needed when you deal with unmanaged objects, locking mechanisms, the operating system (OS) handles in your programs, and so forth. Programmers explicitly need to release those resources. These are the cases where you need to put in special attention to prevent memory leaks. In general, when programmers themselves clean up (or release) the memory, you say that they **dispose** of the objects, but when CLR automatically releases the resources, you say that the garbage collector performs its job. The garbage collector uses the **finalizers** (or, destructors) of the class instance to perform the final cleanup. We'll discuss them shortly.

POINTS TO REMEMBER

Programmers can release resources by explicitly disposing of the objects, or the CLR automatically releases resources through a garbage collection mechanism. We often refer to them as the *disposing* and *finalizing* techniques, respectively.

Stack Memory vs. Heap Memory

To understand the upcoming discussion, it's important to understand the difference between stack memory and heap memory. If you know the difference, you can skip this section. Otherwise, continue reading.

- To execute a program, the operating system gives you a pile of memory. The program splits this into several portions for various uses. There are two major parts; one is stack memory, and the other one is heap memory.

- These two kinds of memories store different kinds of data.

- For example, the stack is used for local variables and to keep track of the current state of the program. What are local variables? They are the variables that are declared in a method.

- By contrast, the instance variables for reference types are stored on the heap. The static variables are stored on the heap too.

- For the reference type variable, the variable itself will be stored on the stack, but the contents are stored on the heap.

- For example, when you see the line A obA=new A();, you understand that the reference variable obA is stored on the stack, but the object/ content is stored on the heap.

The stack follows the last in, first out (LIFO) mechanism. It works like a stack of frames, where one frame is placed on top of another frame. You can also think of it as a set of boxes, where one box is placed on top of another box. All local variables of a particular method can go into a single frame. At a particular moment, you can access the top frame of the stack, but you cannot access the lower frames.

Once the top frame is removed from a stack and discarded, the immediate lower frame can be accessed as it becomes the top frame. The process can continue until the stack is empty. But, in between, the stack size can further increase or decrease during the program execution.

But the most important point is that **the stack-allocated memory blocks are discarded when a method finishes its execution.**

To help you visualize this with simple diagrams, let's consider the following code segment:

```
// The previous code skipped

public void SomeMethod()
  {
    int a=1;// Line-1
    double b=2.5; // Line-2
    int c=3;// Line-3
    // Some other code, if any
  }
}
```

Figure 12-1 shows you four different stages in a single snapshot.

- Assume that the control entered into the method called SomeMethod. The top three lines of this method have been executed, but it does not reach the end of the method body. You can see that the stack is growing in this stage in the first part of this diagram.

- The next parts of the diagram show that the cleaning up of the stack is in progress. It is true that when the control leaves the method body, all the variables a, b, and c are deleted. But following the LIFO structure, I have shown you the intermediate deletions one by one.

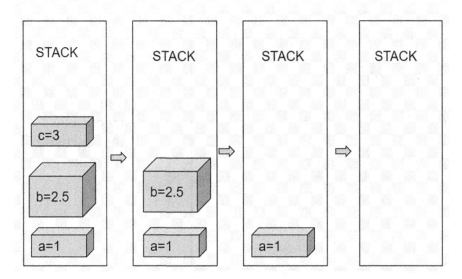

Figure 12-1. *The different statuses of the stack memory when a program runs*

In short, for a stack allocation, you know that once you return from a method, the allocated frame is discarded, and you can use the space immediately.

On the other hand, heap memory is used for object/reference types. Here the tracking of a program state is not the concern. Instead, it focuses on storing the data. A program can easily allocate some space in the heap and start using the space to store the information.

Note   In Visual Studio, in debug mode, you can see the call stack and analyze the stack trace. In addition, once you learn multithreaded programming, you'll see that each thread can have its own stack, but they share the same heap space among them.

For a heap, you can add or remove allocated space in any order. See Figure 12-2.

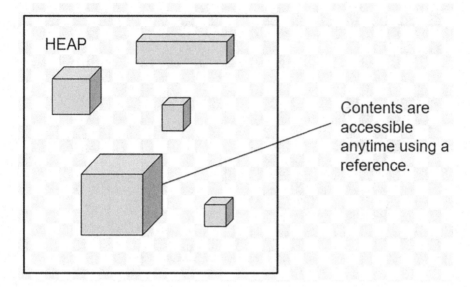

Figure 12-2. *A sample figure that represents a heap memory with different allocations*

In this case, you need to remember the allocation, and before you reuse the space, someone needs to clear the old allocation. But what happens if you forget to delete the space? Or what happens if you use an already created reference to point to a different object in the heap, but later you make it null? These kinds of allocated memory spaces will keep increasing (which becomes garbage), and you'll see the impact of the memory leaks. This is the point where the garbage collector (GC) in C# helps you. Periodically, the GC checks the status and tries to help you by freeing unused spaces.

Each time you create an object, the CLR allocates memory in the managed heap. It can keep allocating the memory until the address space in the managed heap is available. The GC has an optimizing engine to determine when to reclaim unused memories.

Q&A Session

12.1 What is a managed heap?

Answer:
The managed code is the code that is managed by a runtime, e.g., the Common Language Runtime (CLR). This CLR provides many services, and automatic memory management is one of them. When you initialize a process, the runtime reserves a contiguous address space for it. This reserved space is called the *managed heap*.

This managed heap has a pointer that points to the address where the next object will be allocated. You can surely guess that the allocation process for the first object starts with the managed heap's base address. The allocation for the next object will occur to the address that immediately follows the previous object. The garbage collector repeats the process until the address space is available for use.

12.2 I have a solution in my mind. I can allocate memory on the heap, and once my job is done, I'll delete it immediately. This way I can prevent the garbage from growing. Is my understanding correct?

Answer:

Yes, the proposed solution can work and help you prevent leaks. But this is not that easy. There are situations where the objects need to stay alive for a while. Consider an example: using an advanced printer, you simultaneously send multiple emails and faxes to different recipients. At the same time, you start printing some large documents. It is very unlikely that all the recipients receive the data at the same time or a document with a big number of pages is printed instantly. So, an immediate deletion is not a clever solution in these scenarios.

12.3 Let us assume there is a class, called Test. I understand that for the line Test testObj=new Test(); the space for the object will be allocated in the heap memory. But what about the reference variable?

Answer:

The reference variable will stay in the stack memory. See Figure 12-3.

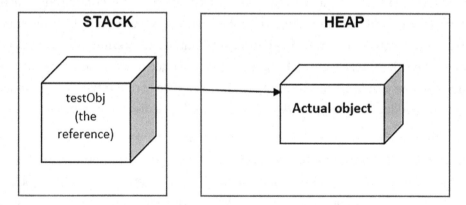

Figure 12-3. *An object reference on the stack points to the actual memory in the heap*

12.4 In many discussions, people say that the struct is on a heap. But my understanding is that the content of a struct should be in the stack. Am I missing something?

Answer:

This is interesting. You have to understand the context. For example, instance variables for a value type are stored in the same context as the variable that declares the value type. So, the `struct` variable that is declared within a method will always be on the stack, whereas a struct variable that is an instance field of a class will be stored on the heap.

12.5 Sometimes I wonder about these references. Are they similar to the pointers in C/C++?

Answer:

The concept is similar, but not the same. Before I answer your question, let me explain something for a better understanding. I already mentioned that the GC manages the heap memory for you. How does it manage this stuff?

- First, it frees up the garbage's/unused spaces for you so that you can reuse the space.

- Second, it can apply the compaction technique, which means it can remove all allocated space to one side of the memory and all the free space to the other side of the memory. It results in contiguous free space that helps you to allocate a large block of memory.

The first point is important and covered in this chapter. The second point is also important because the heap may contain scattered objects (see Figure 12-2). In many situations, you may need to have a big chunk of a contiguous memory that may not available at a particular time, though there is enough space in the heap. In these scenarios, the compaction helps to get enough space. These references are maintained by the garbage collector, and when this kind of shuffling is done, you are not aware of it.

Note   Actually, you have two different types of heap; one is a large object heap (LOH), and another one is a small object heap (SOH). The objects of sizes 85,000 bytes and above are placed in a large object heap. Usually, these are array objects. To make the discussion easy, I simply use the word *heap*, instead of categorizing it. The SOH is used for three different generations, which you'll read in the following section.

To elaborate on these with simple figures, let's assume we have a heap. After the garbage collector's cleanup operation, it may look like Figure 12-4 (white blocks are represented as free/available blocks).

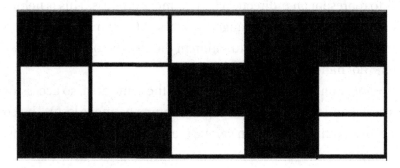

Figure 12-4. *Scattered allocations in the memory before the compaction*

You can see that if you need to allocate five contiguous memory blocks in our heap, you cannot allocate them now, although collectively there are enough spaces. To deal with a similar situation, the garbage collector can apply the compaction technique, which moves all remaining objects (live objects) to one end to form one continuous block of memory. So, after compaction, it may look like Figure 12-5.

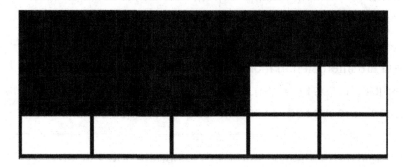

Figure 12-5. *Revised allocations in the memory after the compaction*

Now you can easily allocate five contiguous blocks of memory in the heap. What is the benefit? A new object can be allocated at the end of the contiguous allocation. In programming, you can do this by adding a value to the heap pointer. As a result, you do not need to iterate through a linked list of addresses to find spaces for the new object. In this way, a managed heap is different from an unmanaged heap.

What do I mean by an unmanaged heap? Consider a case when you manage the heap and you are responsible for allocating and deallocating spaces. In simple words, when an object is allocated in a managed heap, instead of getting the actual pointer, you get a "handle" to represent an indirection to a memory address. This is helpful because the actual memory location can be changed after the GC's compaction. But for a native code (say when you use the `malloc()` function in the C/C++ code to allocate a space), you get pointers, not handles.

After the compaction, objects generally stay in the same area, so accessing them also becomes easier and faster (because page swapping happens less). The compaction technique is costly, but the overall gain can be greater. The Microsoft documentation says the following:

> *Memory is compacted only if a collection discovers a significant number of unreachable objects. If all the objects in the managed heap survive a collection, then there is no need for memory compaction.*

> *To improve performance, the runtime allocates memory for large objects in a separate heap. The garbage collector automatically releases the memory for large objects. However, to avoid moving large objects in memory, this memory is usually not compacted.*

Note   If you are interested in more details, I encourage you to read the following .NET blog article: `https://devblogs.microsoft.com/dotnet/large-object-heap-uncovered-from-an-old-msdn-article/`

Now I return to the original question. It is important how you interpret the word *pointer*. In C/C++, using a pointer, you point to an address that is nothing but a number slot in the memory. But the problem is, if you point to an invalid address, you encounter surprises! So, a pointer in an "unsafe" context is tricky.

On the other hand, a reference in C# points to a valid address in the managed heap, or it is null. This is the kind of assurance you receive from C#. In addition, references are useful because when the data moves around the memory, you can access that data using these references.

The Garbage Collector in Action

A generational garbage collector (GC) is used to collect short-lived objects more frequently than longer-lived objects. We have three generations here: 0, 1, and 2. Short-lived objects (for example, temporary variables) are stored in generation 0. The longer-lived objects are pushed into the higher generations—either 1 or 2. The garbage collector works more frequently in the lower generations than in the higher ones.

Once you create an object, it resides in generation 0. When generation 0 is filled up, the garbage collector is invoked. The objects that survive generation 0 garbage collection are transferred to the next higher generation—generation 1. The objects that survive garbage collection in generation 1 enter the highest generation—generation 2. The objects that survive the generation 2 garbage collection stay in the same generation.

POINTS TO NOTE

Sometimes you create a very large object. This kind of object directly goes to the large object heap (LOH). It is often referred to as generation 3. Generation 3 is a physical generation that's logically collected as part of generation 2. In this context, I encourage you to read the online Microsoft documentation at `https://docs.microsoft.com/en-us/dotnet/standard/garbage-collection/large-object-heap` that says the following:

In the future, .NET may decide to compact the LOH automatically. This means that, if you allocate large objects and want to make sure that they don't move, you should still pin them.

I suggest you use the 3-3 rule to remember the different phases of a garbage collection and the different ways to invoke the GC.

Different Phases of Garbage Collection

The following are the three phases of garbage collection:

- **Phase 1**: This is the *marking phase,* in which the live objects are marked or identified.

- **Phase 2**: This is the *relocating phase*, in which it updates the references of the objects that will be compacted in phase 3.

- **Phase 3**: This is the *compacting phase*, which reclaims memory from dead (or unreferenced) objects, and the compaction operation is performed on the live objects. It moves the live objects (that survived until this point) to the older end of the segment.

Different Cases of Invoking the Garbage Collector

The following are three different cases of invoking the garbage collector:

- **Case 1**: You have low memory.

- **Case 2**: The allocated objects (in a managed heap) surpass a defined threshold limit.

- **Case 3**: You call the System.GC() method. There are many overloaded versions of GC.Collect(). The GC is a static class and is defined in the System namespace.

The following program demonstrates a simple case study. I have used the GetTotalMemory() method in this example. I am using the summary from Visual Studio for your immediate reference. The explanation is clear.

```
// Summary:
// Retrieves the number of bytes currently thought to be allocated. A
// parameter indicates whether this
// method can wait for a short interval before
// returning, to allow the system to collect garbage
// and finalize objects.
//
// Parameters:
//   forceFullCollection:
//     true to indicate that this method can wait for
//     garbage collection to occur before
//     returning; otherwise, false.
//
// Returns:
//     A number that is the best available
// approximation of the number of bytes currently
// allocated in managed memory.
```

Similarly, you can see the descriptions of any method from Visual Studio. Here are some brief descriptions of additional methods. I use them in the upcoming example:

- GC.Collect(Int32) forces an immediate garbage collection from generation 0 through a specified generation. This means that when you call Gc.Collect(0), the garbage collection will happen at generation 0. If you call Gc.Collect(1), the garbage collection will happen both at generation 0 and at generation 1, and so forth.

- The CollectionCount method returns the number of times garbage collection has occurred for the specified generation of objects.

- After I invoke the GC, I invoke the WaitForPendingFinalizers() method. This method definition says that this method *suspends the current thread until the thread that is processing the queue of finalizers has emptied that queue.*

- Starting from C# 9.0, you can use a new syntax for a null check. This is shown here. So, the following block of code does not create any compile-time error:

```
if (sample is not null){// some code}
```

- In this program, you'll see the following line:

```
GC.Collect(i, GCCollectionMode.Forced, false,
  true);
```

- At the time of this writing, there are five overloaded methods for Collect():

```
public static void Collect();
public static void Collect(int generation);
public static void Collect(int generation,
  GCCollectionMode mode);
public static void Collect(int generation,
  GCCollectionMode mode, bool blocking);
public static void Collect(int generation,
  GCCollectionMode mode, bool blocking, bool
  compacting);
```

You can see their definitions easily in Visual Studio. For your immediate reference, I present the descriptions here:

> **generation:** This is the number of the oldest generation to be garbage collected.
>
> **mode:** This is an enumeration value that specifies whether the garbage collection is forced (`System.GCCollectionMode.Default` or `System.GCCollectionMode.Forced`) or optimized (`System. GCCollectionMode.Optimized`).
>
> **blocking:** You set this to true to perform a blocking garbage collection; set it to false to perform a background garbage collection where possible.
>
> **compacting:** You set it to true to compact the small object heap; set it to false to sweep only.

The purpose of this example is as follows:

- To show you different generations of garbage collection

- To demonstrate that an object *can* enter from one generation to the next generation if the garbage is not collected

Demonstration 1

Here is the complete demonstration:

```
Console.WriteLine("***Exploring Garbage Collections.***");
try
{
    Console.WriteLine($"Maximum GC Generation is {GC.MaxGeneration}");
    Sample sample = new();
    GCHelper.CheckObjectStatus(sample);

    for (int i = 0; i < 3; i++)
    {
        Console.WriteLine($"\n After GC.Collect({i})");
        GC.Collect(i, GCCollectionMode.Forced, false, true);
        System.Threading.Thread.Sleep(10000);
```

```
        GC.WaitForPendingFinalizers();
        GCHelper.ShowAllocationStatus();
        GCHelper.CheckObjectStatus(sample);
    }
}
catch (Exception ex)
{
    Console.WriteLine("Error:" + ex.Message);
}

class Sample
{
    public Sample()
    {
        // Some code
    }
}

class GCHelper
{
    public static void CheckObjectStatus(
     Sample sample)
    {
        if (sample is not null) // C# 9.0 onwards OK
        {
            Console.WriteLine($" The {sample} object is in Generation:
             {GC.GetGeneration(sample)}");
        }
    }

    public static void ShowAllocationStatus()
    {
        Console.WriteLine("---------");
        Console.WriteLine($"Gen-0 collection
         count:{GC.CollectionCount(0)}");
        Console.WriteLine($"Gen-1 collection
```

```
            count:{GC.CollectionCount(1)}");
        Console.WriteLine($"Gen-2 collection
         count:{GC.CollectionCount(2)}");
        Console.WriteLine($"Total Memory
         allocation:{GC.GetTotalMemory(false)}");
        Console.WriteLine("---------");
    }
}
```

Output

Here is one possible output. I have highlighted some important lines in bold. On your computer, you may see different outputs. Read the "Analysis" section to learn more about this difference.

```
***Exploring Garbage Collections.***
```
Maximum GC Generation is 2
 The Sample object is in Generation:0

```
 After GC.Collect(0)
 ---------
Gen-0 collection count:1
Gen-1 collection count:0
Gen-2 collection count:0
```
Total Memory allocation:154960
```
 ---------
```
 The Sample object is in Generation:1

```
 After GC.Collect(1)
 ---------
Gen-0 collection count:2
Gen-1 collection count:1
Gen-2 collection count:0
```
Total Memory allocation:147624
```
 ---------
```
 The Sample object is in Generation:2

```
After GC.Collect(2)
---------
Gen-0 collection count:3
Gen-1 collection count:2
Gen-2 collection count:1
```
Total Memory allocation:146848
```
---------
```
The Sample object is in Generation:2

POINTS TO NOTE

It is possible to see the different counters if additional garbage collection happens in between these calls. In this possible output, you can see that the sample instance was not collected in any of the GC invocation calls. So, it survived and gradually moved to generation 2.

The total memory allocations in this output seem to be logical because, after each GC invocation, you see that the total allocations are reducing. **This may not happen in every possible output** because you may not allow the GC to complete its job before you show the memory status. So, to get a more consistent result, I also introduced a sleep time, after I invoke the GC, and I also invoke WaitForPendingFinalizers(). This allows the GC to have more time to complete its job. Yes, it causes some performance penalties, but in my system, it produces a more consistent result. Based on your system configuration, you may need to vary the sleep time accordingly.

Notice that I have used the following overloaded version: GC.Collect(i, GCCollectionMode.Forced, false, true). You understand that I make the third parameter false to perform a background garbage collection if possible.

Another important point to note: before a garbage collection starts, all the managed threads are suspended, except the thread that invokes the GC. So, once the GC finishes its task, other threads can start allocating spaces again. If you know the concept of multithreading, understanding the previous line is easy for you.

One last point: these generations are a logical view of the GC heap. Physically these objects reside on the managed heap, which is a chunk of memory. The GC reserves this from the OS via calling VirtualAlloc. We are not going to discuss it in that detail.

Analysis

This is only sample output that can vary on every run. If needed, you can go through the theory in the previous sections again and then try to understand how the garbage collection happened. Here are some important observations:

- There are different generations of the GC.

- You can see that once you called `GC.Collect(2)`, the other generations are also called. Notice that the counters have increased. Similarly, when you called `GC.Collect(1)`, generation 1 and generation 0 both are called.

- You can also see the object that I created was originally placed in generation 0.

Q&A Session

12.6 Can you give examples of short-lived and long-lived objects?

Answer:

Temporary variables are examples of short-lived objects. By contrast, you can consider some objects in a server applications that use some static data throughout a process execution as typical long-lived objects.

12.7 What is the key benefit of having a generation-based garbage collection?

Answer:

Microsoft believes that most of the time we can reclaim enough memory when garbage collection occurs at generation 0. This means we can save time by not working on other generations. Freeing memory from one particular part of memory is faster than inspecting the whole memory area and releasing spaces. It saves time and increases efficiency.

12.8 Why is generation 2 garbage collection called a full garbage collection?

Answer:

Collecting a generation means collecting objects from the current generation and the younger generation. For example, generation 1 collection means collecting objects from generation 1 and generation 0. Similarly, generation 2 garbage collection means collecting objects from generation2, generation 1, and generation 0; that is the full collection from the managed heap.

Disposing of an Object

A programmer often needs to explicitly release some resources. Some common examples include when you work with events, locking mechanisms, file handling operations, or unmanaged objects. There are also cases when you know that you have used a very large block of memory that is not necessary after a certain point of execution. These are some examples where you want to release the memory or resources to improve the performance of your system.

Author's Note   Some common examples of unmanaged objects are seen when you wrap OS resources such as database connections or network connections. We call them *unmanaged* because the CLR cannot manage them. Why? These objects are created outside the .NET runtime.

In C# programming, you have a built-in IDisposable interface with a Dispose() method. When a programmer wants to release the resources, they can override this Dispose() method. It is a recommended practice because you are very much aware when you are about to release the memory. Here is the description for your reference:

```
namespace System
{
    //
    // Summary:
    //      Provides a mechanism for releasing
    //   unmanaged resources.
    public interface IDisposable
    {
        //
        // Summary:
        // Perform application-defined tasks
        // associated with freeing, releasing, or
        // resetting unmanaged resources.
        void Dispose();
    }
}
```

From the previous description, you can see that you can release unmanaged resources using this method.

Finalize vs. Dispose

Each class can have only one finalizer (often called a *destructor*) that cannot be overloaded or inherited. It does not have a modifier, and it does not take any parameter. You cannot call a finalizer directly. It is invoked automatically. You may note that the following signature is reserved for the finalizer of a class:

```
void Finalize();
```

Author's Note   You can define finalizers for a class, but not for a struct in C#.

Here is a sample example that shows the use of a finalizer (or a destructor) inside a parent class and one of its derived classes:

```
class Parent
{
  ~Parent()
   {
    // Cleanup statements are not shown here.
   }
}
    class Child : Parent
    {
        ~Child()
        {
            // Cleanup statements are not shown here.
        }
    }
```

Compile this code segment and then examine the IL code for these classes.

Note   You can use an IL disassembler to see the IL code. I often use `ildasm.`
`exe`, which is automatically available in Visual Studio. To use this tool, you can
follow these steps: open a developer's command prompt for Visual Studio,
type **ildasm** (you can see a new window will pop up), and drag a `.dll` to this
window. Now expand/click the code elements. You can learn more about this tool
at `https://docs.microsoft.com/en-us/dotnet/framework/tools/`
`ildasm-exe-il-disassembler`.

For the Parent class, you'll notice something like the following (I have made some
lines bold for your reference):

```
.method family hidebysig virtual instance void
        Finalize() cil managed
{
  .override [System.Runtime]System.Object::Finalize
  // Code size       13 (0xd)
  .maxstack  1
  IL_0000:  nop
  .try
  {
    IL_0001:  nop
    IL_0002:  leave.s     IL_000c
  }  // end .try
  finally
  {
    IL_0004:  ldarg.0
    IL_0005:  call        instance void
     [System.Runtime]System.Object::Finalize()
    IL_000a:  nop
    IL_000b:  endfinally
  }  // end handler
  IL_000c:  ret
} // end of method Parent::Finalize
```

For the Child class, you'll notice something like the following:

```
.method family hidebysig virtual instance void
       Finalize() cil managed
{
  .override [System.Runtime]System.Object::Finalize
  // Code size        13 (0xd)
  .maxstack  1
  IL_0000:  nop
  .try
  {
    IL_0001:  nop
    IL_0002:  leave.s     IL_000c
  } // end .try
  finally
  {
    IL_0004:  ldarg.0
    IL_0005:  call        instance void
     Demo_Testing_Finalizers.Parent::Finalize()
    IL_000a:  nop
    IL_000b:  endfinally
  } // end handler
  IL_000c:  ret
} // end of method Child::Finalize
```

This IL code reflects the following points:

- You can see that a finalizer invocation implicitly translated to the following:

  ```
  protected override void Finalize()
  {
      try
      {
          // Cleanup statements are not shown
          // here.
      }
  ```

```
finally
{
    base.Finalize();
}
}
```

- The Child class finalizer calls the Parent class finalizer, which in turn calls the Object class finalizer. This means that this method is called recursively for all instances in an inheritance chain, and the direction of the call is from the most specific to the least specific. In short, you understand that the finalizer of an object implicitly calls the Finalize method on the base class of the object.

Note   Microsoft recommends not using empty finalizers. This is because, for a finalizer, an entry is made in the Finalize queue. When a finalizer is called, the GC starts processing this queue. So, if the finalizer is empty, you introduce an unnecessary performance penalty for it.

Let's look at a program where you see the presence of a finalizer and a Dispose() method. Before you run this program, let me tell you about the following points:

- The static class GC is defined in the System namespace.

- This class has a method, called SuppressFinalize(). If you pass the current object in the GC.SuppressFinalize() method, the finalize method of the current object is not invoked.

- I want you to show a destructor invocation in .NET 7. Actually, the result is the same for the .NET core platform (for example in .NET 5, .NET 6, or .NET 7). **In the .NET Framework, it is easy. Once you exit the program, it is called automatically.** But a different logic is implemented in the .NET core platform. This is why I introduce another class, called A, and initialize a Sample object inside the constructor. I also do not use any Sample reference inside Main() before I invoke the GC. This helps the GC to figure out that the Sample object is no longer needed and it can collect the garbage. A similar logic can be implemented to mimic the behavior in the .NET core platform.

Run the following program now to see the output. Then go through the analysis. You need to understand an important design change in the .NET platform.

POINTS TO REMEMBER

Ideally, unless it is required, you do not want to write code in the finalizer. Instead, you may prefer to use the `Dispose()` method to release unmanaged resources and avoid memory leaks.

Demonstration 2

Here is the complete demonstration. I ran it in .NET 7, but this time I did not use top-level statements because I wanted to compare the same program in an older edition (.NET Framework 4.7.2) and the latest editions (such as .NET 5+). Top-level statements have been available since .NET 6.

Note   At the time of this writing, .NET is a common term for .NET Standard and all the .NET implementations and workloads. It is recommended that you use it for all the upcoming development, i.e., for .NET Core and .NET 5, and later versions. It is a cross-platform, high-performance, open-source implementation of .NET. By contrast, .NET Framework is designed only for Windows.

Sometimes you see a plus sign after a version number. This plus sign after the version number means "and later versions." For example, .NET 5+ should be interpreted as .NET 5 and the later/subsequent versions.

```
class Sample : IDisposable
{
    public void SomeMethod()
    {
        Console.WriteLine("Sample's SomeMethod is invoked.");
    }
```

```csharp
    public void Dispose()
    {
        // GC.SuppressFinalize(this);
        Console.WriteLine("Sample's Dispose() is called.");
        // Release unmanaged resource(s) if any
    }
    ~Sample()
    {
        Console.WriteLine("Sample's Destructor is called.");

    }
}
class A : IDisposable
{
  public A()
    {
      Console.WriteLine("Inside A's constructor.");

        //using (Sample sample = new Sample())
        //{
        //    sample.SomeMethod();
        //}
        // Simplified statement (C# 8 onwards it
        // works).
        using Sample sample = new();
        sample.SomeMethod();
    }
    public void Dispose()
    {
        // GC.SuppressFinalize(this);
        Console.WriteLine("A's Dispose() is called.");
        // Release any other resource(s)
    }
```

```
        ~A()
        {
            Console.WriteLine("A's Destructor is called.");
        }
    }
    class Program
    {
        static void Main(string[] args)
        {
            Console.WriteLine("*** Exploring the
             Dispose() method.***");
            A obA = new();
            obA = null;
            Console.WriteLine("GC is about to start.");
            GC.Collect();
            GC.WaitForPendingFinalizers();
            Console.WriteLine("GC is completed.");
            Console.ReadKey();
        }
    }
```

Output

Here is the output when I use .NET Core 3.1, .NET 5, .NET 6, or .NET 7(Preview):

```
*** Exploring the Dispose() method.***
Inside A's constructor.
Sample's SomeMethod is invoked.
```
Sample's Dispose() is called.
```
GC is about to start.
```
Sample's Destructor is called.
```
GC is completed.
```

Analysis

From this output, notice the following points:

- The Sample class object's Dispose() and finalizer method are both called.

- The statement GC.SuppressFinalize(this); is commented in the Dispose() method of the Sample class. **This is why the destructor of the Sample instance was called too. If you enable/uncomment this statement, the finalizer of the Sample instance will not be called.**

- The object's finalizer method has not been called yet.

When I executed the same program in the .NET Framework 4.7.2, I saw an additional line toward the end, which says that A class object's destructor is also called in this case. Here is the output:

```
*** Exploring the Dispose() method.***
Inside A's constructor.
Sample's SomeMethod is invoked.
Sample's Dispose() is called.
GC is about to start.
Sample's Destructor is called.
A's Destructor is called.
GC is completed.
```

Note   I raised a ticket at Microsoft regarding the difference in output when using the .NET Framework and .NET Core. If you are interested to know about this discussion, you can refer to https://github.com/dotnet/docs/issues/24440. Microsoft believes that it is an expected behavior in .NET Core/.NET 5/.NET 6 applications. Different opinions exist as well.

Refer to the Microsoft documentation (`https://docs.microsoft.com/en-us/dotnet/csharp/programming-guide/classes-and-structs/destructors`) that says the following:

> *The programmer has no control over when the finalizer is called; the garbage collector decides when to call it. The garbage collector checks for objects that are no longer being used by the application. If it considers an object eligible for finalization, it calls the finalizer (if any) and reclaims the memory used to store the object.*

In .NET Framework applications (but not in .NET Core applications), finalizers are also called when the program exits. The explanation I got for this is that finalizers could produce a deadlock that prevented a program from exiting. Therefore, the code to run finalizers on exit was relaxed. The following link describes the issue in depth: `https://github.com/dotnet/docs/issues/17463`.

There is updated documentation now. See `https://learn.microsoft.com/en-us/dotnet/csharp/programming-guide/classes-and-structs/finalizers` where Microsoft confirms this behavior by saying the following:

> *Whether or not finalizers are run as part of application termination is specific to each implementation of .NET. When an application terminates, . NET Framework makes every reasonable effort to call finalizers for objects that haven't yet been garbage collected, unless such cleanup has been suppressed (by a call to the library method GC.SuppressFinalize, for example). .NET 5 (including .NET Core) and later versions don't call finalizers as part of application termination.*

Before you move on to the topic of memory leak in detail, let's review our understanding in the following Q& A session.

Q&A Session

12.9 How can we call destructors (or finalizers)?

Answer:
You cannot call a destructor. The garbage collector takes care of that responsibility.

12.10 How can you free up a resource?

Answer:

The garbage collector does this for you. But the GC cannot allocate or free unmanaged resources. So, a programmer tries to use the Dispose() method to release unmanaged resources. To optimize the performance, the programmer may suppress the finalizer call on an object if wanted. In this context, you may see a **dispose pattern**, something like the following:

```
class Sample : IDisposable
{
    bool _disposedAlready = false;
    protected virtual void Dispose(bool disposing)
    {
        // Checking whether the object
        // is already disposed
        if (_disposedAlready)
        {
            return;
        }
        if (disposing)
        {
            // Some code to dispose managed
            // objects
        }
        // Dispose the unmanaged objects
        // and large files(if any) here

        _disposedAlready = true;
    }

    public void Dispose()
    {
        // Dispose the unmanaged resources
        Dispose(true);
        // Suppress the finalizer call
        // to tell: "GC, you do not need
        // to do anything more."
```

263

```
        GC.SuppressFinalize(this);
    }
    ~Sample()
    {
        Dispose(false);
    }
    // Some other code
}
```

POINTS TO REMEMBER

In the previous code segment, note the following points:

- The disposing parameter is false when called from a finalizer. But it is true when you invoke it from the `Dispose` method. In other words, it is true when it is deterministically called and false when it is nondeterministically called. This follows Microsoft's programming guidelines.

- In addition, you must remember that in C# programming, you do not override the `Object.Finalize` method to implement finalization; instead, you provide a finalizer.

- Microsoft suggests that a `Dispose` method should be callable multiple times without throwing an exception.

12.11 When does the garbage collector call the `Finalize()` method?

Answer:

We never know. It may call instantly when an object is found with no references or later when the CLR needs to reclaim some memory. But you can force the garbage collector to run at a given point by calling `GC.Collect()`, which has many overloaded versions. You have seen two different usages already when I used different overloaded versions of `GC.Collect()` in demonstration 1 and demonstration 2.

12.12 Finalizers are called automatically when the program ends in the .NET Framework. But this is not the case in .NET Core or .NET 5 or NET 6. What is the reason behind this?

Answer:

In response to my ticket at `https://github.com/dotnet/docs/issues/24440`, the answer is summarized as follows: finalizers could produce a deadlock that could prevent a program from exiting. Therefore, the code to run finalizers on exit was relaxed. Microsoft believes that it is expected behavior in .NET Core and .NET 5+ applications.

12.13 When should we invoke the GC.Collect()?

Answer:

I already mentioned that invoking the GC is generally a costly operation. But in some special scenarios, if you can invoke GC, you'll gain some significant benefits. Such an example may arise after you dereference a large number of objects in the code.

Another common example is when you try to find memory leaks through some common operations, such as executing a test repeatedly to find leaks in the system. After each of these operations, you may try to gather different counters to analyze memory growth and to get the correct counters. I'll discuss memory leak analysis shortly.

POINTS TO REMEMBER

When we see the use of the `IDisposable` interface, we assume that the programmer will call the `Dispose()` method correctly. Some experts suggest you have a destructor also as a precautionary measure. It can help in a sense when a call to the `Dispose()` is missed. Remember Microsoft's philosophy (see `https://docs.microsoft.com/en-us/dotnet/standard/garbage-collection/implementing-dispose`): to help ensure that resources are always cleaned up appropriately, the `Dispose` method should be idempotent, such that it is callable multiple times without throwing an exception. Furthermore, subsequent invocations of `Dispose` should do nothing.

12.14 Why did you use using statements in the previous demonstration (demonstration 2)?

Answer:

C# provides special support in this context. You can use the `using` statement to reduce your code size and make it more readable. ***It is a syntactic shortcut for the try/finally block***. To verify this, you can see the IL code for the A's constructor that I used in demonstration 2. Some portions are bold for your reference.

```
.method public hidebysig specialname rtspecialname
        instance void   .ctor() cil managed
{
  // Code size        46 (0x2e)
  .maxstack   1
  .locals init (class Demo2_NonTLS_Version.Sample V_0)
  IL_0000:  ldarg.0
  IL_0001:  call        instance void
   [System.Runtime]System.Object::.ctor()
  IL_0006:  nop
  IL_0007:  nop
  IL_0008:  ldstr       "Inside A's constructor."
  IL_000d:  call        void [System.Console]
   System.Console::WriteLine(string)
  IL_0012:  nop
  IL_0013:  newobj      instance void
   Demo2_NonTLS_Version.Sample::.ctor()
  IL_0018:  stloc.0
  .try
  {
    IL_0019:  ldloc.0
    IL_001a:  callvirt    instance void
     Demo2_NonTLS_Version.Sample::SomeMethod()
    IL_001f:  nop
    IL_0020:  leave.s     IL_002d
  }  // end .try
  finally
  {
    IL_0022:  ldloc.0
    IL_0023:  brfalse.s  IL_002c
    IL_0025:  ldloc.0
    IL_0026:  callvirt    instance void
     [System.Runtime]System.IDisposable::Dispose()
    IL_002b:  nop
    IL_002c:  endfinally
```

```
  }  // end handler
  IL_002d:  ret
} // end of method A::.ctor
```

12.15 Can I directly allocate spaces in generation 1 or generation 2?

Answer:

No. A user code can allocate spaces in generation 0 or LOH only. It is the GC's
responsibility to promote an object from generation 0 to generation 1 (or, generation 2).

12.16 Can I overload a finalizer?

Answer:

As I told you earlier, the following signature is reserved for the finalizer of a class:

```
void Finalize();
```

What does this mean? It does not accept any parameter. As a result, a finalizer cannot
be overloaded. This implies that a class can have at most one finalizer.

Summary

Memory management is an important topic. This chapter gave you a quick overview
of this topic, but still, it is a big chapter! We began with a quick discussion about the
importance of memory leaks. Then you saw how the memory is managed in C#.

I started the discussion about two different types of memory in C#, such as stack
memory and heap memory. Then I discussed the garbage collector in C#. You saw
different phases of garbage collection and learned different cases in which a GC can start
its operation.

Then you learned about disposing of an object programmatically. You saw a
discussion on the `Dispose` method versus the finalizer method. And in this case, you saw
how the .NET Framework shows a different behavior than .NET Core or .NET 5+. Finally,
you learned about the `Dispose` pattern that is often used in this context.

In short, this chapter answered the following questions:

- How is a heap memory different than a stack memory?

- What is garbage collection? How does it work in C#?

- What are the different GC generations?

- What are the different ways to invoke the garbage collector?

- How can we force GC to invoke?

- How does the disposing differ from finalizing in C#?

- How can you implement a dispose pattern in your program?

CHAPTER 13

Analyzing Memory Leaks

Before we discuss memory leaks, let's analyze a simple case study. It will help you understand how memory leaks can hamper the smooth execution of an application over the long run. Suppose you have an online application where users need to fill in some data and then click the submit button. We can assume that during this process, you need to use some resources that consume some blocks of computer memory. Obviously, once the process is completed, developers release the allocated blocks of memory. Now assume that unfortunately the developers of the application mistakenly forgot to deallocate some blocks during the process of execution. Because of this misjudgment, let's say that the application leaks 512 bytes per click. You probably won't notice any performance degradation from some initial clicks. But what happens if thousands of online users use the application simultaneously? If 1,000,000 users click the submit button, the application will eventually cause 488 MB of memory loss. You cannot allow this for a long time, because if it goes like this, the application becomes slower and slower, and in the worst case, the application can crash. These are common symptoms caused by memory leaks.

This is why in the previous chapter I told you that if a computer program runs over a long time but fails to release memory resources, you may face some challenging situations like the following:

- A machine becomes slow over time.

- A specific operation in an application takes longer to execute.

- The worst case is that an application/system can crash.

In short, even if a program leaks a small amount of data for a common operation, it is quite obvious that you will see some kind of malfunction over time; for example, your device may crash with a `System.OutOfMemoryException`, or operations in the device may become so slow that you need to restart the application often. It is apparent that "**how fast it comes to your attention**" **depends** on the **leaking rate** of the application.

© Vaskaran Sarcar 2023
V. Sarcar, *Simple and Efficient Programming with C#*, https://doi.org/10.1007/978-1-4842-8737-8_13

Managed vs. Unmanaged Memory Leaks

I hope that you read Chapter 12 carefully. There you learned that if you work with C++, you are responsible for the memory deallocations. But in the case of C#, the CLR plays a big role, and most of the time it helps you not to worry about the deallocations.

Still, there are situations when you need to take the responsibility for deallocations. For example, in the case of handling events, you need to be careful: if you register an event, you need to unregister it. This book is about C#, so we'll discuss managed memory leaks, and to illustrate this, I'll use events.

I assume that you know how to use events in an application. A detailed discussion of events and delegates is beyond the scope of this book. However, I have added some supportive comments in the code to help you understand it a little better. I acknowledge that it may be easy for you to find the problem in this program. But my core intention is to show you how to analyze the event leaks using the diagnostic tools in Visual Studio. The Diagnostic Tools window can help analyze CPU and memory usage. Here you can view events that show performance-related information.

Note   I discuss delegates, events, and other topics in detail in my other books, *Interactive C#* and *Getting Started with Advanced C#*, also published by Apress. The first book shows the usage of the diagnostic tools as well as Microsoft's CLR Profiler to analyze memory leaks. The second one discusses delegates and events in depth. Also, my recent book *Test Your Skills in C# Programming* covers these topics. So, if you are interested, you can take a look at those books.

Before I show you how to use the diagnostic tool, I want you to recall that you can programmatically find the current memory consumption of a program's objects using the GetTotalMemory method. I used this method in demonstration 1 of Chapter 12 as follows:

```
Console.WriteLine($"Total Memory allocation:
  {GC.GetTotalMemory(false)}");
```

You may wonder why I did not pass the true argument, because it tells the GC to perform a collection first. The answer is that I found that introducing the sleep time in that program helped me to get a more consistent result rather than purely relying on this true parameter. Let me pick the parameter description from this method description for your immediate reference. The following description also does not guarantee that the collection will be completed before you see the result.

```
// Parameters:
//   forceFullCollection:
//       true to indicate that this method can wait for
//       garbage collection to occur before
//       returning; otherwise, false.
```

So, since I could not rely on the true parameter, I made it false in that program.

Memory Leak Analysis

Now the question is, how can you detect leaks? Let me tell you that finding a memory leak in an application is a challenging task! There are many tools for this purpose. For example, windbg.exe is a common tool to find memory leaks in a large application. In addition, you can use other graphical tools, such as Microsoft's CLR Profiler, SciTech's Memory Profiler, Red Gate's ANTS Memory Profiler, and so forth to find the leaks in your system. Many organizations have their company-specific memory leak tools to detect and analyze leaks. In my previous organization, our experts developed such a tool. It is a wonderful tool. I was fortunate because I used it for several years and learned many interesting things about catching memory leaks.

Visual Studio users can use a variety of profiling tools for diagnosing different kinds of app performance issues depending on the app type. In the latest editions of Visual Studio, you can see a Diagnostic Tools window. It shows you the profiling tools that are available during a debugging session. You can use it to detect and analyze memory leaks. It is very user-friendly and easy to use. Using this tool, you can take various memory snapshots. Markers in the tool indicate garbage collector activities. These are very useful and effective: you can analyze the data in real time while the debugging session is active. The spikes in the graph can draw your attention immediately. The following program shows you a sample demonstration.

Before you run this application, ensure that you enable the option to launch the Diagnostic Tools, as shown in Figure 13-1. In the Visual Studio IDE, you can see this option in Tools ➤ Option ➤ Debugging ➤ General.

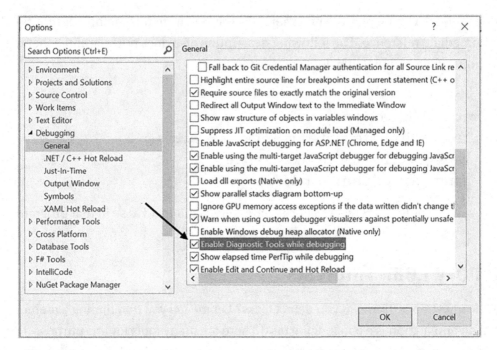

Figure 13-1. *Enabling the "Diagnostic Tools while debugging" option in Visual Studio Community 2022*

If you do not see this option on your machine, you can **launch the Visual Studio Installer**, click the **Modify** button, go to the **Individual Component** tab, and then check whether you have installed the profiling tools on your machine. Figure 13-2 shows you an example.

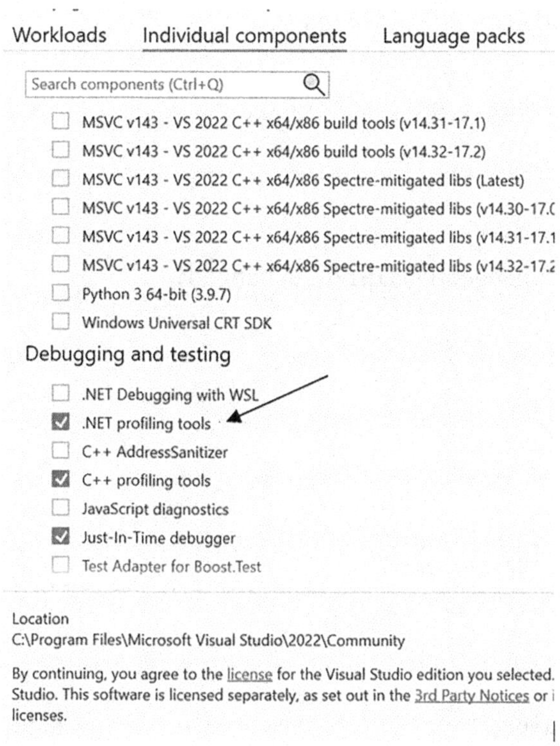

Figure 13-2. *Checking whether .NET profiling tools are installed in the machine*

Demonstration

Here is the complete demonstration. Inside the client code, you'll see two methods: one to register the events and one to unregister the event. You can see that by mistake, I have registered too many events, but I have unregistered only one of them. And these remaining events will cause leaks in this application.

```
Console.WriteLine("***Creating custom events and
  analyzing memory leaks.***");
Sender sender = new();
Receiver receiver = new();
Helper.RegisterNotifications(sender, receiver);
Helper.UnRegisterNotification(sender, receiver);

delegate void IdChangedHandler(object sender,
  IdChangedEventArgs eventArgs);
```

```
class IdChangedEventArgs : EventArgs
{
    public int IdNumber { get; set; }
}
class Sender
{
    public event IdChangedHandler? IdChanged;

    private int Id;
    public int ID
    {
        get
        {
            return Id;
        }
        set
        {
            Id = value;
            // Raise the event
            OnMyIntChanged(Id);
        }
    }

    protected void OnMyIntChanged(int id)
    {
      if (IdChanged != null)
       {
          // It is the simplified form of the
          // following lines:
          // IdChangedEventArgs idChangedEventArgs =
          //   new IdChangedEventArgs();
          // idChangedEventArgs.IdNumber = id;

          IdChangedEventArgs idChangedEventArgs = new()
           {
               IdNumber = id
           };
```

```
        //if (IdChanged != null)
        //{
        //    IdChanged(this, idChangedEventArgs);
        //}

        //Simplified form
        IdChanged?.Invoke(this, idChangedEventArgs);
    }
  }
}
class Receiver
{
    public void GetNotification(object sender,
     IdChangedEventArgs e)
    {
        Console.WriteLine($"Sender changed the id
          to:{e.IdNumber}");
    }
}
class Helper
{
    public static void RegisterNotifications(Sender
     sender, Receiver receiver)
    {
        for (int count = 0; count < 10000; count++)
        {
            // Registering too many events.
            sender.IdChanged += receiver.GetNotification;
            sender.ID = count;
        }
    }
    public static void UnRegisterNotification(Sender
      sender, Receiver receiver)
    {
```

```
        // Unregistering only one event.
        sender.IdChanged -= receiver.GetNotification;
    }
}
```

I ran this program and start taking different snapshots when the program is running. (If you do not see the Diagnostic Tools window, you can bring up the window from **Debug ➤ Windows ➤ Show Diagnostic Tools** or press **Ctrl+Alt+F2**). Figure 13-3 shows the Diagnostic Tools window; it includes five different snapshots to analyze memory usage at a given point in time.

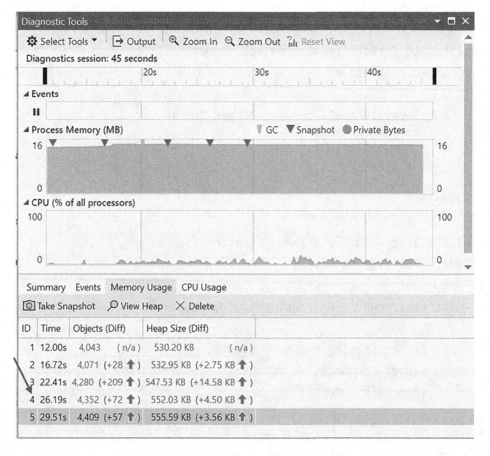

Figure 13-3. *Different snapshots are taken using the Diagnostic Tools in Visual Studio*

Snapshots from Diagnostic Tools

Let's analyze the difference (shown in the column Objects (Diff)). For example, let me pick the row that is associated with ID 4. This row shows the objects count increased by 72 compared to the previous snapshot. If you hover your mouse on this, it will indicate that you can open the heap diff view for the selected snapshot sorted by object count. Let's click this link. See Figure 13-4.

Managed Memory						Compare With Baseline: S
Filter types 🔍 ✓ Show Just My Code ☐ Collapse small object types						
Object Type	Count Diff.	Size Diff. (Bytes)	Inclusive Size Diff. (Bytes)	Count	Size (Bytes)	Inclusive Size (Bytes)
⚙ PreAllocatedOverlapped	0	0	0	2	64	208
⚙ IdChangedHandler	+72	+4,608	+9,216	443	32,472	60,632
⚙ EventCommandEventArgs	0	0	0	5	440	840
⚙ Random	0	0	0	1	24	72
⚙ ReaderWriterCount	0	0	0	1	48	48
Total	+72	+4,608		988	462,816	

Paths To Root Referenced Types		
Object Type	Reference Count Diff.	Reference Count ▲
⊿ ⚙ IdChangedHandler		
⊘ IdChangedHandler [Local Variable]	0	3
⊘ IdChangedHandler [Local Variable]	+72	440

Figure 13-4. *The object count difference in a particular snapshot*

We can see how the heap size is growing over time. See that `IdChangedEventHandler` is causing the damage. Now you can recognize from the code that by mistake, I am registering an event repeatedly inside the `for` loop in this code:

```
sender.IdChanged += receiver.GetNotification;
```

Actually, I have placed the `for` loop in the wrong place. I needed to remove it from the `RegisterNotifications` method. Instead, I needed to place this loop inside the client code as follows:

```
Console.WriteLine("***Creating custom events and
  analyzing memory leaks.***");
Sender sender = new();
Receiver receiver = new();
```

277

```
for (int count = 0; count < 10000; count++)
{
    Helper.RegisterNotifications(sender, receiver);
    sender.ID = count;
    Helper.UnRegisterNotification(sender, receiver);
}
// The remaining code is skipped
```

Similarly, I could show you the leak using Microsoft's CLR profiler. But showing the usage of different tools is not the aim of the chapter. Instead, you want to prevent memory leaks using any tool you like. Since the diagnostic tool is already available in the latest editions of Visual Studio, I do not want to miss the opportunity to show its usage.

I want to tell you that catching a memory leak needs expertise because it is not very easy. In the previous demonstration, our program has a few methods; that is why it is easy to catch the leak. But think about some typical scenarios:

- You use third-party code that has a leak. However, you cannot immediately find it, because you do not have access to the code.

- Let's assume that the leak can be revealed when some specific code path is followed. If the test team misses that path, it'll be hard to find the leak.

- A dedicated memory leak suite maintenance may need a separate test team. Also, you cannot include all the regression tests in the memory leak suite. It is simply because running a test multiple times and gathering those counters are both time-consuming and resource-consuming activities. So, it is recommended that you shuffle the test cases often and run your memory leak test suite.

- When a new bug fix takes place, a test team verifies the fix using some test cases. Now you need to ask them whether those tests are already included in the memory leak test suite. If not, you need to include them. But if multiple fixes come in one day (say 10 or more), what to do? It may not be possible for you to include all the tests in your memory leak suite due to various reasons (for example, you may have resource constraints). Also, since a memory leak suite needs to run for hours, you get to see the result much later. So, in between, if new fixes enter into the main codebase, it is very hard to catch a leak that came earlier.

Summary

Preventing memory leaks in an application is a challenging task. It requires expertise and patience to find a leak in an application. In this chapter, I showed you the Diagnostic Tools window in Visual Studio and how to analyze a memory leak using events in C#.

This chapter answered the following questions:

- What is a memory leak?

- Why should you be careful about memory leaks?

- What are the probable causes of memory leaks?

- How can you perform a memory leak analysis with Visual Studio's Diagnostic Tools window?

CHAPTER 14

More Tips

This is the last chapter of the book. Earlier I told you that sometimes it's OK to bend some well-accepted rules for your application if it performs well, but when you keep coding and developing applications, you'll find that the experts' suggestions have great value. If you follow their advice, you'll understand that a simple choice can have a big impact in the long run. This chapter discusses some of these topics in brief.

Learn Design Patterns

Let's take a tour with a time machine to the early days of software development to understand the following common problem in those days:

There is no standard to instruct developers on how to design an application. We are unique creatures. So, each corporate team follows its own style of coding. A new member joins such a team. Understanding the current architecture is a gigantic task for this member. So, he is continually seeking help from the senior members of the team and requesting that they explain the existing architecture. He keeps asking them: why do you follow this particular design in this code segment? The experienced developer answers his question. This experienced developer also explains why the common alternatives were not considered in a previous team meeting. She also suggests that the new member reuse the existing construct to reduce future development efforts.

What is the problem with this scenario? Actually, there is no problem; this is standard practice, even in today's world. But think about it from a different perspective. Let's say the experienced developer tells the new member, "We follow the Facade pattern for this code segment" or "We follow the Singleton pattern in that code segment." If the new team member already knows about these patterns of coding, how much easier will that make it? Since he knows these styles of coding, following a known pattern, it's easy for him to contribute to the team quickly. I hope this scenario gives you some idea about the importance of knowing some standard patterns.

© Vaskaran Sarcar 2023
V. Sarcar, *Simple and Efficient Programming with C#*, https://doi.org/10.1007/978-1-4842-8737-8_14

Software design patterns address this kind of issue and provide a common platform for all developers. You can think of them as the recorded experience of experts in the field. These patterns were originally intended to be applied in object-oriented designs with the intention of reuse.

Brief History of Design Patterns

The original idea of design patterns came from building architect Christopher Alexander, a professor at Berkeley. He faced many problems that were similar in nature. So, he tackled those issues with similar kinds of solutions.

> *Each pattern describes a problem, which occurs over and over again in our environment, and then describes the core of the solution to that problem, in such a way that you can use this solution a million times over, without ever doing it the same way twice.*
>
> *Christopher Alexander*

His original ideas were for a building's construction within a well-planned town. Later these concepts entered the software engineering community. This community started believing that though these patterns were described for buildings and towns, the same concepts could be applied in object-oriented design. So, they substituted the original concepts of walls and doors with objects and interfaces. The idea was the same: you can apply a known solution to a common problem.

These concepts started gaining popularity through leading-edge software developers like Ward Cunningham and Kent Beck. In 1994, the idea of design patterns entered the mainstream of object-oriented software development through an industry conference called Pattern Languages of Program Design (PLoP) on design patterns. It was hosted by the Hillside Group, and Jim Coplien's paper "A Development Process Generative Pattern Language" is a famous one in this context.

In addition, in 1994, Erich Gamma, Richard Helm, Ralph Johnson, and John Vlissides published the book *Design Patterns: Elements of Reusable Object-Oriented Software* (Addison-Wesley, 1994). In this book, they introduced 23 design patterns for software development. These authors became known as the Gang of Four. We often refer to them as the **GoF**. You can easily guess that the patterns they talked about were developed by the common experiences of software developers over a period of time.

It is important to note that the GoF discussed the design patterns in the context of C++. C# 1.0 was released in 2002, and then it went through various changes. It grew rapidly and secured its rank as the world's top programming languages within a short period, and in today's market, it is always in high demand. At the time of this writing, C# 11.0 is about to be released. Since the concepts of design patterns are universal, they are always valuable. So, exercising the fundamental design patterns makes you a better programmer and helps you to make a better version of your program.

Here are some important points to remember:

- A design pattern describes a general reusable solution to software design problems. The basic idea is that while developing software, you can solve similar kinds of problems with similar kinds of solutions. The proposed solutions were tested over a long period.

- Patterns are actually templates. They suggest to you how to solve a problem. A good understanding of patterns can help you to implement the best possible design much faster.

- From an OOP perspective, these patterns are descriptions of how to create objects and classes and customize them to solve a general design problem in a particular context.

Each of the 23 GoF design patterns focuses on a particular object-oriented design. Each of them can describe the consequences and trade-offs of use. The GoF categorized these 23 patterns based on their purposes, as shown here:

Creational Patterns:

These patterns abstract the instantiation process. You make the systems independent of how the objects are composed, created, and represented. Here you ask: "Where should I place the new keyword in my application?" This decision can help you determine the degree of coupling of your classes. The following five patterns belong to this category:

- Singleton pattern

- Prototype pattern

- Factory Method pattern

- Builder pattern

- Abstract Factory pattern

Structural Patterns:

Using these patterns, you combine the classes and objects to form a relatively large structure. Normally you use inheritance or composition to group different interfaces or implementations. In Chapter 7, you saw that preferring object composition over inheritance (and vice versa) can affect the flexibility of your software. The following seven patterns fall into this category:

- Proxy pattern

- Flyweight pattern

- Composite pattern

- Bridge pattern

- Facade pattern

- Decorator pattern

- Adapter pattern

Behavioral Patterns:

These patterns focus on algorithms and the assignment of responsibilities among objects. Here you concentrate on the object's communication and its interconnection. The following 11 patterns fall into this category:

- Observer pattern

- Strategy pattern

- Template Method pattern

- Command pattern

- Iterator pattern

- Memento pattern

- State pattern

- Mediator pattern

- Chain of Responsibility pattern

- Visitor pattern

- Interpreter pattern

The Good News

I have some good news for you. You have already implemented some of these patterns! Not only that, you actually learned at least one pattern from each category. Part III of this book helps you understand them.

- In Chapter 6, you learned about the Factory Method pattern. In fact, you also learned the simple Factory pattern, which is the foundation of this pattern.

- In Chapter 7, you learned about the Decorator pattern.

- In Chapter 8, you learned about the Template Method pattern.

- In Chapter 9, you learned about the Facade pattern.

In addition

- Chapter 2 in Part I created a foundation for the Strategy pattern.

- Chapter 11 in Part IV discussed the non-GoF patterns called the Null Object pattern and the Special Case pattern.

These patterns are common in C# applications. Congratulations! You are on the right path.

Q&A Session

14.1 Can I combine two or more patterns in an application?

Answer:
Yes, in real-world scenarios, this type of activity is common.

14.2 Do these patterns depend on a particular programming language?

Answer:
Programming languages can play an important role. But the basic ideas are the same. Patterns are just like templates, and they give you some idea in advance about how to

solve a problem. Instead of any object-oriented programming language, suppose you have chosen some other language like C. In that case, if you follow object-oriented programming, you need to implement the core object-oriented principles such as inheritance, polymorphism, encapsulation, abstraction, and so on. So, the choice of a particular language is important, because it may have some specialized features that can make your programming life easier.

14.3 Should I consider the common data structures like arrays and linked lists also as different design patterns?

Answer:

The GoF clearly excludes those saying that *they are not complex, domain-specific designs for an entire application or subsystem.* They can be encoded in classes and reused as is. So, they are not design patterns in this context.

14.4 If no particular pattern is 100 percent suitable for my problem, how should I proceed?

Answer:

An infinite number of problems cannot be solved with a finite number of patterns for sure. But if you know these common patterns and their trade-offs, you can pick a close match. Lastly, no one prevents you from using a pattern for your own problem. But you have to tackle the risk, and you need to think about your return on investment.

Remember that the world is always changing, and new patterns keep evolving. To understand the necessity of a new pattern, you may also need to understand why an old (or existing) pattern is not enough to fulfill the requirement. These patterns attempt to make a solid foundation for you. These concepts can help you move smoothly in your professional life.

Avoid Anti-patterns

The design patterns can help you make better applications. They have been developed and tested over time. So, in general, using them is considered a good practice. But often people misuse them and cause more trouble. The anti-patterns point to those bad practices and warn you. Here is a common example: a developer implements a quick fix without analyzing the potential pitfalls or skips the test cases to meet a delivery schedule. Now think about the company's reputation if a customer finds a big bug due to that quick fix.

Anti-patterns alert you in similar situations and help you to take precautionary measures. They remind you of the proverb "Prevention is better than the cure."

POINTS TO REMEMBER

Anti-patterns not only warn about common mistakes but also suggest better solutions. Some of these solutions may not be attractive at the beginning, but in the long run, they save your time, effort, and reputation.

Brief History of Anti-patterns

Undoubtedly, the ideas of design patterns helped (and are still helping) millions of programmers. Gradually people started noticing the negative impacts due to the tendency to overuse these patterns. For example, say many developers wanted to show their expertise without the true evaluation or consequences of these patterns in their specific domains. As an obvious side effect, patterns were implanted in the wrong context, produced low-quality software, and ultimately caused big penalties to them or their organizations.

So, the software industry needed to focus on the negative consequences of similar kinds of mistakes, and eventually, the idea of anti-patterns evolved. Many experts started contributing to this field, but the first well-formed model came through Michael Akroyd's presentation entitled "AntiPatterns: Vaccinations against Object Misuse." It was the antithesis of the GoF's design patterns. Wikipedia says the term was coined in 1995 by computer programmer Andrew Koenig. Martin Fowler, a well-known author and speaker in the software industry, also believes this. The term *anti-pattern* became popular with the book *Anti Patterns: Refactoring Software, Architectures, and Projects in Crisis* (Robert Ipsen/Wiley). This book says the following:

> *"Because AntiPatterns have had so many contributors, it would be unfair to assign the original idea for AntiPatterns to a single source. Rather, AntiPatterns are a natural step in complementing the work of the design pattern movement and extending the design pattern model."*

Examples of Anti-patterns

These are some examples of the anti-patterns and the concepts/mindsets behind them:

- *Overuse of Patterns*: Developers may try to use patterns at any cost, regardless of whether they are appropriate.

- *God Class*: A big object controls almost everything with many unrelated methods.

- *Not Invented Here*: I am a big company, and I want to build everything from scratch. Though there is a library that was developed by a small company, I will not use it. I will make everything of my own, and once it is developed, I'll use my brand value to announce: "Hey, we are here to provide you the ultimate library to fulfill your every need."

- *Zero Means Null*: A programmer may use some special numbers, such as -1 or 999 (or anything similar) to represent an inappropriate integer value. A similar example can be seen when a programmer treats something like "09/09/9999" as a null date in an application. In these cases, if the user needs to have these values, they will not get them.

- *Golden Hammer*: Mr. X believes that technology T is the best. So, if he needs to develop a new system (that demands new learning), he will still prefer T even if it is inappropriate. He thinks, "I am old enough and quite busy. I do not need to learn any more technology if I can somehow manage it with T."

- *Shoot the Messenger*: You believe that the tester "Josie" always finds hard defects for you because she does not like you. You think you're already under pressure, and the program deadline is approaching. So, you do not want her to be involved in this crucial stage to avoid more defects.

- *Swiss Army Knife*: A company targets a product that can serve every need of a customer. Imagine that a company tries to make a drug that can cure all illnesses. Or, someone wants to design software that can serve a wide range of customers with varying needs. It does not matter to the concerned person how complex the interface is.

- ***Copy-and-Paste Programming***: This is when you need to solve a problem, but you already have a piece of code to deal with a similar situation. So, you can take a copy of the old code that is currently working and start modifying it if required. But when you start from an existing copy, you essentially inherit all the potential bugs associated with it. Also, if the original code needs to be modified in the future, you need to implement the modification in multiple places. This approach violates the don't repeat yourself (DRY) principle.

- ***Architects Don't Code***: Say you are an architect. Your time is valuable, so you only show paths or give great lectures on coding. There are enough implementers who should implement your ideas. *Architects Play Golf* is also a sister of this anti-pattern.

- ***Disguised Links and Ads***: This comes from a mindset that is fooling users and earning revenue when they click a link or an advertisement. Often the customer does not get what they really want. We call them **dark patterns**.

- ***Management by Numbers***: Someone may believe that a larger number of commits, a larger number of lines of code, or a larger number of defects fixed, etc., is a sign of a great developer.

I'll finish this discussion with an interesting quote that suits perfectly in this discussion.

Measuring programming progress by lines of code is like measuring aircraft building progress by weight.

Bill Gates (`https://www.goodreads.com/quotes/536587-measuring-programming-progress-by-lines-of-code-is-like-measuring`)

```
                     POINTS TO NOTE
```

- You can learn about various anti-patterns from different sources. For example, the following Wikipedia page talks about various anti-patterns: `https://en.wikipedia.org/wiki/Anti-pattern`.

- You can also read the anti-pattern catalog at `http://wiki.c2.com/?AntiPatternsCatalog` to learn more.

- The concept of anti-patterns is not limited to object-oriented programming.

Q&A Session

14.5 How are anti-patterns related to design patterns?

Answers:

When you use design patterns, you reuse the experiences of others who came before you. When you start blindly using those concepts for the sake of use only, you fall into the trap of *reusing recurring solutions*. This can lead you to a bad situation in the future, and then you identify that your return on investment (ROI) keeps decreasing, but maintenance cost keeps increasing. In simple words, if you are not careful enough, then an apparently easy and attractive solution (or, pattern) may cause more problems for you in the future.

14.6 A design pattern may turn into an anti-pattern. Is the understanding correct?

Answers:

Yes, if you apply a design pattern in the wrong context, it can cause more trouble than the problem it solves, and eventually it will turn into an anti-pattern. So, before you start, understanding the nature and context of the problem is very important. For example, inappropriate use of the Mediator pattern may end up with a God Class anti-pattern.

14.7 Anti-patterns are related to software developers only. Is the understanding correct?

Answers:

No. You have already seen various types of anti-patterns. So, the usefulness of an anti-pattern is not limited to developers; it may apply to others also. For example, they can be useful to managers and technical architects too.

14.8 Even if you do not get much benefit from anti-patterns now, these can help you to adapt new features easily with fewer maintenance costs in the future. Is the understanding correct?

Answers:

Yes.

14.9 What are the probable causes of anti-patterns?

Answers:

Anti-patterns can come from various sources or mindsets. A few common examples of what someone might say (or, think) are listed here:

- "We need to deliver the product as soon as possible."

- "We have a very good relationship with the customer. So, at present, we do not need to analyze much about the future impact."

- "I am an expert on reuse. I know design patterns very well."

- "We will use the latest technologies and features to impress our customers. We do not need to care about legacy systems."

- "More complicated code will reflect my expertise in the subject."

14.10 Can you mention some symptoms of anti-patterns?

Answers:

In object-oriented programming (OOP), the most common symptom is that your system cannot adopt a new feature easily. Also, maintenance cost is continuously increasing. You may also notice that you have lost the power of key object-oriented features like inheritance, polymorphism, etc.

In addition, you may notice some or all of the following symptoms:

- Use of global variables

- Code duplication

- Limited/no reuse of code

- One big class (God class)

- Presence of a big number of parameters-less methods

14.11 What is the remedy if you detect an anti-pattern?

Answers:

You may need to refactor your code and find a better solution. For example, here are some solutions to avoid the following anti-patterns:

- *Golden Hammer*: You may try to educate Mr. X through some proper training.

- *Zero Means Null*: You can use an additional Boolean variable that is more sensible to you to indicate the null value properly.

- *Management by Numbers*: Numbers are good if you can use them wisely. But you cannot judge the ability of a programmer only by the number of defects fixed per week. Quality is also important. A typical example is that fixing a simple UI layout is much easier compared to fixing a critical memory leak in the system. Consider another example. "More tests are passing" does not indicate that your system is more stable unless these tests exercise different code paths/branches.

- *Shoot the Messenger*: Welcome tester "Josie" and involve her immediately. Don't consider her as a rival of you. You can properly analyze all of her findings and fix the real defects early to avoid last-moment surprises.

- *Copy-and-Paste Programming*: Instead of searching for a quick solution, you can refactor your code. You can also make it commonplace to maintain the frequently used methods to avoid duplicates and easier maintenance.

- *Architects Don't Code*: Involve architects in some parts of the implementation phase. It can help both the organization and themselves. This activity can give them a clearer picture of the true functionalities of the product. And truly, they should value your effort.

14.12 What do you mean by refactoring?

Answers:

In the coding world, the term *refactoring* means improving the design of existing code without changing the external behavior of the system/application. This process helps you to get more readable code. At the same time, this code should be more adaptable to new requirements (or, change requests), and they should be more maintainable.

Final Suggestions

Before I end this chapter, let me share some of my thoughts with you.

Decide Between a Static Method and an Instance Method

A static method is easy to use. A novice programmer may think that it does not matter much whether they use a static method or an instance method in their program. They know that they can call a method without instantiating an object. They love this and are further impressed when they see some static utility methods that are extremely helpful. But an experienced programmer often finds it interesting and decides whether they should use a static method or not. In each possible design, the programmer may ask, which of them is better? The short answer is that there is no universal rule. I believe that it purely depends on the application you use. Let us verify the fact.

Remember the simple factory (demonstration 1) in Chapter 6? See Figure 14-1.

```
class AnimalFactory
{
    2 references
    public IAnimal CreateAnimal(string animalType)
    {
        IAnimal animal;
        if (animalType.Equals("cat"))
        {
            animal = new Cat();
        }
        else if (animalType.Equals("tiger"))
        {
            animal = new Tiger();
        }
        else
        {
            Console.WriteLine("You can create either a cat or a tiger. ");
            throw new ApplicationException("An unknown animal cannot be instantiated.");
        }
        return animal;
    }
}
```

Figure 14-1. *The AnimalFactory class from demonstration 1 in Chapter 6*

If you investigate the arrow tip, you see the message in Figure 14-2.

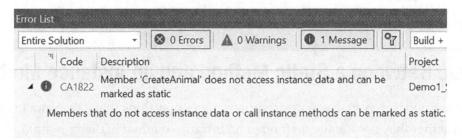

Figure 14-2. *A message that says you can use a static method instead of an instance method*

This is a partial snapshot; I am expanding the full message for you:

CA1822 Member 'CreateAnimal' does not access instance data and can be marked as static.

It also says the following:

> Active Members that do not access instance data or call instance methods can be marked as static. After you mark the methods as static, the compiler will emit nonvirtual call sites to these members. This can give you a measurable performance gain for performance-sensitive code.

Note   I can see this suggestion when I set the target framework to .NET 7, .NET 6, or .NET 5. But it is not visible when I use .NET 3.1 as my target framework.

I did not take this suggestion in Chapter 6. The reason is obvious.

- You cannot mark a static method with virtual or abstract keywords.

- As a result, you cannot override a static method. So, you cannot use the override keyword either.

- When you cannot redefine a method using the override keyword, you do not get polymorphic behavior.

- In Chapter 6, I enhanced the initial implementation and deferred some responsibilities to subclasses. This was because I wanted to implement the polymorphic behavior. When you predict that you may need to do the same for your application, it's better to make the method nonstatic.

Let me summarize the key points for you:

- If you use a method that can get all the information from its parameters and does not operate on any instance of a class, you can make the method static. For example, look at the following Utility class with the static method ShowGreater:

```
class Utility
{
    public static double ShowGreater(
        double first,
        double second)
    {
        return first >= second ? first : second;
    }
}
```

It makes sense to me to use it as Utility.ShowGreater(24.7, 75.2) to print the greater number between 24.7 and 75.2. It is unnecessary to create an instance of Utility before you print the maximum between 24.7 and 75.2. You can refer to the built-in Math class to get an idea about good static methods. For example, using Math.Max(2,3), you can get 3, or using Math.Abs(-2.52), you can get 2.52.

- If you do not want to see polymorphic behavior or you care only about the performance of your application, you can consider making your method static.

- Sometimes you see partial code, and then you feel that a static method makes more sense to you. But you have seen that you may need to enhance your program in the future, so you apply the concept of polymorphism to make your code flexible. Whenever you are in doubt, prefer a nonstatic method over its counterpart (i.e., a static method).

Know the Common Terminology

You learn continuously. You can read articles, develop new code, discuss problems, and learn from others. To do so, you need to understand common terminology. In this section, I'll remind you of some of them.

Starting with a good design is important, but maintaining it is equally important. If we focus on quick fixes without maintaining the original design goals or architecture, we'll create more troubles for us. This is the reason that an inappropriate design can make an application **rigid**. Even if you start with a good design, the continuous quick fixes to this application can make it inefficient. A simple change may demand lots of effort. In the worst case, you see the **fragility** issue. What does this mean? In simple words, one small change in one location causes changes in multiple locations, and in the worst case, you discover that some of these areas are in no way related to the original change request.

You can develop applications quickly if you reuse some built-in parts that you or someone else developed earlier. When an entry-level programmer hears about reuse, they think that **inheritance** is the best possible option in every possible scenario, but that is not true. You have seen that in many situations object **composition** offers a better solution than inheritance. But the use of inheritance, or composition, becomes secondary if you use a code segment that is dependent on many other things, or already has potential errors. The inability to reuse software is often termed **immobility**.

Viscosity is another important thing to consider in OOP. Wikipedia describes it as the ease at which a developer can add design-preserving code to a system. If you can add new code to your program easily, your program has a low viscosity. The opposite is obvious: in a high-viscosity design, adding hacks is easy, instead of preserving the original design. You can surely predict that by providing these hacks you make your system more rigid. This is one form of viscosity, which is also referred to as the **viscosity of design**.

Note   Adding new code while preserving the core design requires expertise. The word *hack* in the previous context is used to mark an inelegant or bad solution. This solution with a hack can inefficiently serve the purpose. Here I am not talking about the hackers who can find loopholes and security breaches in a system. Once they find those loopholes, they can use their talents either for good purposes or for bad purposes. But undoubtedly, those are programmers with exceptional skills.

There is a different form, called **viscosity of environment**. Consider a case when developers use a pillar build before they push a change in the main codebase. What do I mean by a *pillar build*? Suppose your company has developed a large application that has many components or modules. I refer to them as *pillars*. Since these components are big, to maintain separate components, the company may employ separate teams. Each team has a facility: they can compile a specific pillar using a special command to ensure that a new change in the pillar does not break other parts of the same pillar/component. This is a pillar build. So, you can think of it as a single module build or a single component build. It is attractive when the full build (i.e., the complete compilation of all pillars) is a time-consuming activity, but you need to verify a fix as soon as possible. I do not need to tell you that purely relying on this kind of pillar build is risky if you work on interconnected modules.

Cohesion and **coupling** are two more important concepts that were invented by Larry Constantine in the late 1960s. What do we mean by *cohesion*? The dictionary's meaning of cohesion is interconnection or unity. In OOP, when you design a class, it measures the strength of the relationship between a class's method and data. It will be easy for you if you can remember the single responsibility principle (SRP) in Chapter 4. These concepts go hand in hand, though cohesion is a more general concept.

The opposite is coupling. Wikipedia says that *coupling* is the degree of interdependence between software modules. In OOP, it is a measure of interdependence between two classes. Say there are two separate classes: A and B. Now consider the case when A uses a B object in one of its methods, or you create a B class object inside the A class constructor and work on that. In these cases, A and B are tightly coupled. Even if B is a subclass of A and uses A's method, you can say that they are tightly coupled. Remember that you should aim for high **cohesion** and low **coupling**. I finish this section with Robert C. Martin's words from "The Clean Code Blog" (`https://blog.cleancoder.com/uncle-bob/2014/05/08/SingleReponsibilityPrinciple.html`):

If you think about this (SRP) you'll realize that this is just another way to define cohesion and coupling. We want to increase the cohesion between things that change for the same reasons, and we want to decrease the coupling between those things that change for different reasons.

Accept Failures!

As software developers, we are continuously developing new functionalities or features. When the test team validates them, you will see that lots of tests have failed. For example, if a test suite contains 100 test cases, the result may show **pass, pass, fail, pass, fail, fail, fail, pass, fail, fail, and so on**. This is quite natural. But I have seen that often people like to see only "passes," not the failures. Ask any expert about this. These mean that you have done good so far; now you'll need to fix the failing scenarios one by one. Just like introducing bad code in one part of the software can create many bugs, the opposite is also true! A fix in one place can fix many problems in other places. In fact, if I do not see any test failures with my initial development, I doubt the strength of the test suite. You should not forget the hard truth: your job is to produce good-quality software, not to produce code that passes every test in a test suite.

Q&A Session

14.13 You have used top-level statements throughout the second edition of this book. Is there any specific reason?

Answer:

The honest answer is that I can type less, the code size is small, and I can get the desired output without a problem. Consider the following code:

```
using System;

namespace UsingTopLevelStatements
{
    class Program
    {
        static void Main(string[] args)
        {
```

```
        Console.WriteLine("Hello World!");
      }
    }
}
```

In earlier versions of C# and .NET, the namespace and the `args` parameter were optional. Starting with .NET 5, you can have a further simplified version, shown here:

```
using System;
```

```
Console.WriteLine("Hello World!");
```

Author's Note   Remember that to compile this you have to use C# 9.0 (target framework .NET 5.0); otherwise, you will see the following: `Error CS8400 Feature 'top-level statements' is not available in C# 8.0.`

When I started writing code for this second edition of the book and targeting .NET 7, I could see that I did not need to mention the namespace. How is that possible? Starting with .NET 6 SDK, we have a set of *implicit* global `using` directives for certain projects. These implicit directives include the most common namespaces for the project type. You can see that everything is done behind the scenes!

For example, now I can write a one-liner and compile the following code:

```
Console.WriteLine("Hello, World!");
```

Note that in .NET 5, you'll the following error for this one-liner code (without the namespace):

```
Error CS8773 Feature 'global using directive' is not available in C# 9.0.
Please use language version 10.0 or greater.
```

So, it's a big simplification. This feature is useful for scripting scenarios too. I agree that today if a beginner starts with this shortcut, it can be hard to imagine the background stuff and the legacy code. (But it is possible that after a few years, all beginners will prefer to start from here.)

14.14 I have read your other books. It appears to me that you always focus on design, not on the latest features. Is there any specific reason for this?

Answer:

We all know that change is the only "constant" in the software industry. Whatever is new today will be outdated tomorrow. Most of the time, you work with a legacy version to support existing customers. Unless the company decides you should work on an update, you keep fixing the bugs in the legacy versions too. So, I always try to keep a balance. In my other books, I also use the fundamental features of a programming language and focus on the program design so that you can learn about the design changes easily. This is the main reason I prefer to write code that is supported in a wide range of versions.

14.15 Do you suggest any general advice for me?

Answer:

I like to follow in the footsteps of senior programmers and teachers who are experts in this field. Here are some general suggestions from them:

- Program to a supertype (abstract class/Interface), not an implementation.

- Except for a few cases, prefer composition over inheritance wherever you can.

- Try to make a loosely coupled system.

- Segregate the code that is likely to vary from the rest of your code.

- Encapsulate what varies.

Summary

Following in the expert's footprints and learning from experience is a good strategy. Therefore, understanding design patterns is important. At the same time, it is recommended that you use them wisely; otherwise, you will notice the impact of anti-patterns. As an obvious effect, you need to invest your time to refactor the code or implement a new design starting from scratch. At any cost, you should prefer an unattractive, better fix over an attractive quick fix.

I also described some common terminologies and shared some of my thoughts with you at the end of this chapter. I believe that you'll find them helpful in the future.

APPENDIX A

Winning Notes

Congratulations! You have reached the end of the journey. Anyone can start a journey, but only a few will complete it with care. So, you are among the minority who possess the extraordinary capability to cover the distance successfully. I hope that you have enjoyed your learning experience, which can help you to learn and experiment further in this area. If you repeatedly think about the discussions, examples, implementations, and Q&A sessions in the book, you will have more clarity about them, you will feel more confident about them, and you will remake yourself in the programming world.

What is next? You should not forget the basic principle that *learning is a continuous process*. So, this book was an attempt to encourage you to learn some fundamental concepts so that you can continue learning in more depth.

I also suggest you participate in open forums and join discussion groups to get more clarity on this subject. This process will not only help you; it will help others also.

A Personal Appeal to You

Over the years, I have seen a general trend in my books. When you like the book, you send me messages, write nice emails, and motivate me with your kind words and suggestions. But most of these messages do not reach review platforms like Amazon and others. I only see criticisms on those pages.

I want to assure you that I know these criticisms help me to write better. But it will be helpful for me to know what you like about a book as well. These constructive suggestions can be included in an updated edition of the book.

So, I have a request for you: You can always point out the improvement areas of this work, but at the same time, please let me know what you liked about this book, and let others know about it in reviews. In general, it is always easy to criticize, but an artistic view and open mind are required to discover the true efforts that are associated with any kind of work. Thank you, and happy coding!

© Vaskaran Sarcar 2023
V. Sarcar, *Simple and Efficient Programming with C#*, https://doi.org/10.1007/978-1-4842-8737-8

APPENDIX B

Resources

This appendix lists some useful resources. Some of them are my books, and some of them use a different programming language. You can benefit from these books or their updated editions:

- *Design Patterns in C#: A Hands-on Guide with Real-world Examples* by Vaskaran Sarcar (Apress, 2018)

- *Clean Architecture: A Craftsman's Guide to Software Structure and Design* by Robert C. Martin (Pearson, 2017)

- *The Pragmatic Programmer: From Journeyman to Master by Andrew Hunt and David Thomas* (Addison-Wesley Professional, 1999)

- *Design Patterns: Elements of Reusable Object-Oriented Software* by Erich Gamma et al. (Addison-Wesley, 1995)

- *Interactive C#: Fundamentals, Core Concepts, and Patterns* by Vaskaran Sarcar (Apress, 2017)

- *Head First Design Patterns* by Eric Freeman and Elisabeth Robson (O'Reilly, 2004)

- *Getting Started with Advanced C#: Upgrade Your Programming Skills* by Vaskaran Sarcar (Apress, 2020)

- *The C# Player's Guide (Third Edition)* by RB Whitaker (Starbound Software, 2017)

The following are helpful online resources. These links are working fine at the time of this writing:

- https://dotnet.microsoft.com/learn/dotnet/what-is-dotnet

- https://docs.microsoft.com/en-us/dotnet/csharp/programming-guide/classes-and-structs/finalizers

© Vaskaran Sarcar 2023
V. Sarcar, *Simple and Efficient Programming with C#*, https://doi.org/10.1007/978-1-4842-8737-8

- https://docs.microsoft.com/en-us/dotnet/csharp/whats-new/csharp-9

- https://docs.microsoft.com/en-us/dotnet/csharp/whats-new/csharp-11

- https://docs.microsoft.com/en-us/dotnet/csharp/whats-new/breaking-changes/compiler%20breaking%20changes%20-%20dotnet%207

- https://blog.cleancoder.com/uncle-bob/2014/05/08/SingleReponsibilityPrinciple.html

- https://docs.microsoft.com/en-us/dotnet/standard/garbage-collection/fundamentals

- https://docs.microsoft.com/en-us/dotnet/csharp/language-reference/language-specification/basic-concepts#automatic-memory-management

- https://devblogs.microsoft.com/dotnet/large-object-heap-uncovered-from-an-old-msdn-article/

- https://docs.microsoft.com/en-us/dotnet/standard/garbage-collection/unmanaged

Index

A

AbcCompany, 114
AboutGame() method, 112, 117
AboutMe() method, 23
Abstract class, 6, 15, 18
    centralized behavior, 38
    default method, 97
    fields, 29, 33
    implementation, 33
    vs. interface, 21–23, 26, 28
    output, 36
    Vehicle, 31
Abstraction IDatabase, 102, 103
Abstract method, 172
AdditionalPrice property, 158, 159
AddPlayground() method, 160
AdvancedPrinter, 90, 94
Agile Principles, Patterns and Practices in C# (book), 53
Airplane class, 25, 27
AnimalFactory class, 134, 135, 137, 146, 293
Animal hierarchy, 22, 140
AnimalProducer class, 10
AnimalProducer.MakeSound(animal), 13
Anti-patterns, 300
    architects don't code, 289, 292
    copy-and-paste programming, 289, 292
    disguised links and ads, 289
    examples, 291
    god class, 288
    golden hammer, 288, 292
    history, 287
    management by numbers, 289, 292
    not invented here, 288
    overuse of patterns, 288
    precautionary measures, 287
    shoot the messenger, 288, 292
    sources, 290
    swiss army knife, 288
    zero means null, 288, 292
args parameter, 299
ArtsDistinctionDecider, 71
Asset class, 188, 189
Attributes, 45

B

BasicGameInfo.Game, 124
BasicGameInfo project reference, 123, 124
BasicHome class, 154
BasicPrinter, 90, 97
Behavioral patterns, 284, 285
Boat class, 25
BufferedStream class, 166, 167
BuildHome() method, 158, 160, 166
Built-in comments, 48
Bus object, 220

C

C#, 236, 265
C# 1.0, 283
C# 11.0, 283

© Vaskaran Sarcar 2023
V. Sarcar, *Simple and Efficient Programming with C#*, https://doi.org/10.1007/978-1-4842-8737-8

H

I, J, K

L